HELP MY
UNBELIEF

WILLIAM J. O'MALLEY

ORBIS BOOKS

Maryknoll, New York 10545

Copyright © 2008 by William J. O'Malley.

Published by Orbis Books, Maryknoll, New York 10545–0308.

Manufactured in the United States of America.
Manuscript editing and typesetting by Joan Weber Laflamme.

Library of Congress Cataloging-in-Publication Data

O'Malley, William J.
    Help my unbelief / William J. O' Malley.
        p. cm.
    Includes bibliographical references.
    ISBN-13: 978-1-57075-803-4
    1. Apologetics. 2. Faith. 3. Atheism. I. Title.
    BT1103.O48 2008
    239—dc22

2008009324

For
Millie and Bill Hall

CONTENTS

Introduction

RETHINKING CERTITUDES

> *So many unanswered questions live within me,*
> *afraid to uncover them—because of the*
> *blasphemy. If there be God—please forgive me.*
> *When I try to raise my thoughts to heaven—*
> *there is such convicting emptiness that those*
> *very thoughts return like sharp knives*
> *and hurt my very soul.*[1]
> —MOTHER TERESA

"The fool says in his heart, 'There is no God'" (Ps 14:1). On the other hand, anyone who says he or she hasn't the slightest hesitation about yielding total acceptance to a God who some very, very smart people have said can't exist, isn't too nimble-minded either.

Several years ago I had a mutually enjoyable e-mail correspondence with a paleo-anthropologist who had also written a fine futuristic novel that wrestled expertly with many of the God questions. But then I sent her a chapter I'd written about what insights the ordinary educated person might find into God from science, especially from the purposefulness that seemed to emerge from the design of so much of the universe. Mistake. She rocketed right through the Van Allen Belt, snapping that I ought to leave such questions to people who knew what they were talking about, "people with academic degrees." Ever since, I've felt shamed by my presumption. The seed of this book began to germinate when I resolved instead to lessen my ignorance, at least

1

in some significant way, and to establish definitively (at least for myself) that there's no subject one can't learn more about—most assuredly the God who baffled even Aquinas.

For one thing, there are precious few conclusions I haven't the faintest doubt about. One is "We'll all die." Another is "Bricks released out the window will go down." Almost everything else ranges from "Well, I have *hardly* the slightest doubt" all the way to "Give me a *break*, will ya?"—with the numbers thickening rapidly as we move from one side to the other. "This is the stock to buy—the career for me—the spouse for my life" are all chancy. Water will always freeze at 32° F.—*provided* no one's slipped in anti-freeze. "I will wake up tomorrow." Well, I'm, uh, pretty much counting on it. There's a chance the person Socrates never existed; everything we know about him comes through Plato and his friends. Who says you can trust even history books? Didn't you see *The Matrix*?

Being at least somewhat uncertain is a quite fitting position to take on nearly every serious question. What's more, it avoids the sin of blasphemy (even when one's certitude claims the unyielding backing of the church), since absolute certitude is the prerogative only of God. Saint Peter, the very first pope, publicly admitted he'd been dead wrong about two elements of the Christian faith he'd thought were unalterable: circumcision and the Jewish dietary laws (Acts 2:41; 10:9–16, 44–48; 15:13–22). Saint Paul, the first one after Jesus to interpret his message (even before the Gospels were written), had been sublimely confident in his role as hunter of Christians: "circumcised on the eighth day, of the people of Israel, of the tribe of Benjamin, a Hebrew of Hebrews; in regard to the law, a Pharisee; as for zeal, persecuting the church; as for legalistic righteousness, faultless" (Phil 3:5–6). Until Jesus waylaid him on the road to Damascus (Acts 9).

We tend to forget that even *Jesus* was tempted to believe he might have been wrong! ("My God! My God, why have you abandoned me?" [Mt 27:45]) The intentions of God are so evidently biased toward evolution and growth that doubt appears to be a prerequisite of fulfilling God's will, since doubt is a hunger for better answers than we contented ourselves with till now.

Mother Teresa of Calcutta—probably the one person in history to be nearly canonized by worldwide common consent of the faithful (and even unbelievers)—was beset by doubts every day for the last fifty years of her life! (Chapter 1)

The two fundamental questions each of us faces are (1) Who am I? and (2) Where do I fit into all this? Who is this person "I"—stripped of all the influences I didn't choose myself? And what is my value and mission at the center of the web of relationships that eddies out from my self into my family, my neighborhood, my work, the nation, the whole human family, the mystifying universe, and beyond (I trust) into the life of the Trinity?

A large part of who each of us is emerges in the ways we resemble other animals, but more important, in the specific ways and potentials by which we differ from all other creatures: the abilities to understand and to empathize. We can learn from others who have shared our humanity over the last three thousand years and been skilled enough to distill their wisdom into books, both sacred and secular, so that we don't have to learn *all* the lessons from scratch and can save ourselves at least a few scars. And this question—who am I?—is yet another that God seems to have created us to remain ever restless with. Unexpected challenges built right into our lives are evidence God doesn't want us to settle too long with insights even into our own souls. (Chapter 2)

The second question—where do I fit into all this?—is really the search for a *myth*, a sense of an established, coherent background against which to find meaning amid all those unexpected intrusions. We need a sense that our lives have a story line, rather than random bits of "this happened to me, and then that, and then that." We can't survive long in a Dali landscape with no consistent landmarks. That's what "family"and "home" did for us for so long before, like Hansel and Gretel, we had to be nudged from the nest to discover our own "home." (Chapter 3)

Before we even examine the core of the Christian myth, peripheral questions can also cause nagging doubt. The primary evidence we have for its truth is the scriptures. Some will say, rightly, that the church is an equally potent guarantee of that truth. However, the validity of the church's claims depends on the prior trustworthiness of those scriptures. There are well-educated people who claim the scriptures are, from beginning to end, no more than primitive stories that clumsily fabricate a background myth accessible to the simple. How true—that is, dependable— are those books? The perpetually grumpy Yahweh? A dry canyon opening up in the Red Sea? Walking on water? Exorcizing demons? More cogently, even in English the scriptures are as baffling as Shakespeare. Also, the four Gospels differ from one another. Why—if all of them were allegedly "inspired" by the same God? Further, "people" now say all the Gospels weren't written till at least a generation after the events. How do I know they weren't trumped up like a P. T. Barnum hoax? How could monotheistic Jews like Thomas say to Jesus, "My Lord and my God" (Jn 20:28)? When I was a kid and heard all this for the first time, I admit I *was* "born yesterday." But I'm not that gullible anymore. (Chapter 4)

All I recall of my early Christian training seems to boil down to "do good and avoid evil." Be kind to the less fortunate, don't hurt anybody, and don't take too much pleasure in *anything* (especially not sex). Is that all they hanged Jesus for? Trying to make us nice and "un-bad"? Does pursuing those goals make decent atheists Christian? If the Christian gospel doesn't unnerve you more than that, you've never really even remotely understood it. The distillation of all that *Christian* means emerges pretty inescapably from the parable of the prodigal son, the beatitudes, the last supper, Jesus' description of the last judgment, and quintessentially in Jesus' death and resurrection. Jesus died because, if he hadn't, he couldn't rise, and "if Christ has not been raised, your faith is futile" (1 Cor 15:17). Simple as that. And how reliable is our evidence to substantiate that? Whatever Jesus exhorted us in word and action to imitate depends, entirely, on those two truths. They are *the* reason a thinking Christian is willing to give love even when "I get nothing out of it." (Chapter 5)

Perhaps the most insistent source of difficulty in accepting the Catholic Church is the church itself. Not a few have, in varying degrees, a perhaps even unacknowledged anger at an institution they see as patriarchal, dismissive, overly erudite, and callously disconnected. In the very first place: why organized religion at all? If the word *religion* means "connection," I can connect to God out in the woods. Also, wise brokers know that, when the management is at odds with itself, don't invest. The church is so riddled with antagonisms, it's a wonder it hasn't exploded. More, for the last two thousand years, the organized Roman Catholic Church has been directly and indirectly responsible for atrocities that would have made Jesus weep. How can a good tree gestate such insidious fruit? Finally (though there are lots more strong objections, but none so blatant), anyone with the slightest understanding of honest love and sexuality and life commitment would balk at accepting an institution that consistently and adamantly decreed that sex between two parents impeded by artificial birth control would, *ipso facto*, sever their connection with the God of Jesus Christ. (Dig yourself out of *that* one! Chapter 6)

Even less-than-perfect responses to all those questions might satisfy "ordinary folks," the sort of people the late Leona Helmsley said were the only ones who pay taxes. But what of those of us who read *Newsweek* and the *New York Times Magazine* every week and do the crossword, in ink, without reaching for a dictionary? "People with academic degrees." We can (pretty much) fathom articles by intimidatingly learned and articulate people like Richard Dawkins, Christopher Hitchens, Sam Harris, and Carl Sagan, who have little more tolerance for all this God-talk than a benign sneer. (And how often does any periodical above the level of *The Reader's Digest* offer an article like "Why a Scientist Believes in God"?) Without a doubt, those well-published atheists are a *lot* smarter than just about anybody who corralled us into belief in God—much less Christianity or Catholicism. Shouldn't someone who claims to be fairly well educated be at least slightly embarrassed to offer praise and confess sins to a Personage who's quite possibly not even there? (Chapter 7)

Finally, the argument against God that is pretty close to a knockout punch: How could a good God allow . . . For a shaky believer, the fact of unmerited suffering can seem like the ace of trump. How could an allegedly kind God permit a universe where innocents suffer? How could an even moderately intelligent God allow freedom to an inadequately evolved tribe of apes? Is there anything that can explain why unmerited suffering occurs and what could justify it? If we claim we believe in a God who is Love, why is it that the only explanation of innocent suffering must trace itself back to a God who is vindictive—not only about an individual's sins but about the contagion inflicted on all the children of a fictional couple?

Give me less-than-totally-inadequate answers to those questions, and I just might take the risk of believing.

1

1

THE NEED FOR CERTAINTY

*Faith is the great cop-out, the great excuse to
evade the need to think and evaluate evidence.
Faith is belief in spite of, even perhaps because of,
the lack of evidence. . . . Faith, being belief that
isn't based on evidence, is the principal vice
of every religion.*[1]
—RICHARD DAWKINS

"I love you with all my heart!"

"Prove it!"

"Well, I, uh. . . ."

How can anyone *prove* love? How can you convince someone
that what you claim is reliably true even if it's not visible, tangible, measurable? How render the other so secure that he or she
is compelled to admit an intangible fact as unarguable? Accepting death in another's place is pretty solid evidence, but it does
preclude any further developments in the relationship. The gift
of sex is one of the most vulnerable acts a human can offer. But
people were using sex as a bargaining chip or a cynical ploy or
a weapon even before they had money. "Oh, I've sacrificed *everything* for you, without holding *anything* back. But *far* be it
from me to remind you how much you owe me!" And there are
poor, sad fools who really accept that as proof—on both sides!

The overwhelming majority of what we claim to believe is
simply *not* based on thorough examination of all available evidence, leading to a cautious, personally forged conclusion. What
we call *my* opinions, in the preponderance of cases, really come

7

secondhand from parents, pals, brokers, teachers. We take it on faith that the daily papers, magazines, and news readers are not making it all up as they go. I personally can tell the Latin diplomas on my doctor's wall don't say "Beware!" But I take it on trust there's a solid reason when she says she has to cut me open. I've never personally been to China, but I take it on faith it's not a conspiracy of cartographers with some hidden agenda. I accept it as reasonable that there are footprints in the moondust, that the pictures we all saw were not shot in a Hollywood studio. The atomic and hydrogen bombs are enough to convince me there are some very potent realities I'm simply not capable of experiencing directly.

Even articulate and sophisticated atheists like Sam Harris and Richard Dawkins manifest an admirable faith they are clearly unaware of. Harris declares that, when we finally find the roots of happiness in the physical brain, "there is every reason to believe" all ethical systems will prove to be no more than electrochemical exchanges. Dawkins writes: "Scientific beliefs are supported by evidence, and they get results. Myths and faiths are not and do not." Which pretty much negates the differences between Thomas More and Henry VIII.

Far too often, people describe faith as "a blind leap in the dark," which is sheer idiocy. Giving ten grand to a guy at the door offering buildable lots in Florida is a blind leap. Marrying your college roommate's sister sight unseen is a blind leap. Betting your paycheck on a horse with your mother's name is a blind leap. Still, when most people say, "Well, I just take it on faith," they really mean, "I don't *know*, all right? So get outta my face!"

We give children confident warnings: "Never take candy from strangers. . . . Eat your vegetables. . . . You're heading for trouble, young lady!" We have no special insight into the future, but most of us have still-sensitive scars from the past. We've been around the track often enough to have a treasury of well-grounded generalizations about probable outcomes. Not certainty, but a dependably high degree of assurance. If you want a verdict from a jury, the very best you can hope for is a decision "with no *reasonable* doubt." If you ask professional scientists for "proof," they will invariably give you an answer that has "very high probability." To ask for something more foolproof than that is (unwittingly) blasphemous. Only God has such certitude.

Theology is what we *know* about the God questions; belief is what we *accept* as true of what we know; religion is what we *do* about what we claim to believe. And what we do is a more authentic indicator of what we really believe than what we claim. I may know (from school, sermons, reading) the church's position on artificial birth control for committed couples, but, putting it together with what I know from biology, psychology, and the history of the controversy, I may come to an honest disbelief in that assertion. And my practice follows my honest, reasoned belief. Further, I may know the church's condemnation of abortion and (even if I differ on some cases, like an hour after a rape) sincerely accept as inescapable that abortion is killing a clearly "human entity." But when my unmarried daughter becomes pregnant, I may find my belief too severely tested to live up to what I honestly believe. That is what the sacrament of reconciliation is for—for what Saint Peter clung to, even after Jesus' trial, and Judas could not.

A real problem with faith for people who approach midlife is that what they know about the God questions (their theology) is, to be honest, limited to what they were able to assimilate years ago as undergraduates or even younger. Since then, their need-to-know has yielded to more pressing questions about their jobs, their families, their financial survival. As a result, their beliefs are often flimsy or even (except perhaps for birth control) no more personally examined than those of adolescents or children. Perhaps an embarrassing admission, but unless we begin from the unvarnished truth we end up skidding in self-delusive circles.

WHOSE TRUTH?

Socrates insisted that the first step toward the truth is humility. The truth is, incontestably, "out there" before I can claim any valid subjective grasp of it. Things tell me what they are and how

I can legitimately use them—not the other way round. Despite the fact that the majority of folks once believed the earth was flat, the planet did not level out to accommodate to their opinion. You are free to treat gin like ginger ale, but sooner or later "the way things are" will prove your opinion wrong. If you choose, you can walk off the Sears Tower. But only once.

An act of faith is an *opinion*. Seeing is not believing, it's *knowing*. Belief is accepting something as true without overwhelming certitude—an opinion based on objective evidence (out there, independent of me) and honest reasoning (unadulterated by biases, wishes, preconditions, propaganda, slapdash thinking) but with no pretensions to absolute closure. In the best of all possible worlds, no one would call anything "*my* opinion" until it was as near as possible to "*the* truth." More often than not, the most honest response to a request for an opinion is, "In this case, I really don't have one worth hearing." But no one likes to appear irresolute.

The very first step to a reliable opinion is to *perceive* (see, hear, touch, smell, taste) what's actually out there, to gather the evidence. A poem, for instance, is not a Rorschach test: What does this make me think of? Rather, what is the *poet* trying to convey, not what stream-of-consciousness does it provoke? If you've forgotten your glasses, your opinion of the Venus de Milo is hardly noteworthy. If you believe Jesus disdained wealthy people or that God holds grudges, you've misread the Gospels. Everybody on the street has an opinion about welfare, homosexuality, the church, and who should be president, but you wouldn't go broke offering a buck to everyone who has honestly studied the questions.

The second step is to evaluate and categorize what you've encountered, to "warehouse" it correctly. What kind of entity is it—animal, vegetable, mineral? It tells me. A forensic pathologist can deduce pretty reliably whether a fetus is human or chimp. If the atoms of this solution are two hydrogen to one oxygen, it tells me it's water; if it's two of each, it's hydrogen peroxide. Like water, I can drink it straight, but I will then expel it—whether I like that or not. If I see a woman lurching down the street, I might guess she's drunk. But if she's actually an epileptic, oh, the difference to her. I can't justly label a boy queer merely because I've seen him throw a baseball awkwardly.

The third step is to put all the best of the carefully analyzed evidence into a logical sequence (an outline) showing the relationships among all the parts, sifting out the core issues into a hierarchy of importance and substantiating each with evidence. To be quite blunt: If you don't know how to outline, you don't know how to think. (To evaluate the crucial value of a painstaking outline, consider the last "I make it up as I go" homily you've heard.)

The fourth step is to formulate a temporarily satisfactory conclusion—one's own personally validated opinion, which remains open to revision (as every other stage of the process should be).

And finally, if you're prudent, offer it to someone whose mind you respect for a critique.

Although no one may have told you at the time, that was what undergirded the whole process of your basic education. Once you achieved fundamental literacy and computation skills, the specific data the teacher believed was crucial day by day proved eminently forgettable. (Who other than math teachers factor equations? Who reads Latin? All that memorizing wasn't to equip us to make a living on "Jeopardy.") The data was no more important in itself than the paper Canon and Xerox use to improve their machines. The whole purpose of basic education—as opposed to mere schooling at one end and to true learning at the other—is training minds to come to trustworthy decisions, to form valid opinions. Quite simply, that is the scientific method, which is as requisite for theology, belief, and religion as for physics.

Perhaps that was a needless digression, but it seemed prudent to lay that foundation. If we manipulate our opinions to suit our own predilections, as relativists do, if it's all up to the individual, then no further discussion is necessary—or even logically possible. Further, if (as many atheists argue) there is no objective truth "out there," independent of our minds and desires, and if there is actually no dimension to our existence that outlives death, then we're all on the deck of *The Titanic,* and it hardly matters how we kill our brief time before annihilation. Mother Teresa and the downtown pimp receive exactly the same "reward": obliteration.

The most gifted unbelievers realize life is too often unbearable without some kind of context in which to judge our worth. Even the most resolute admit it helps us keep slogging onward if we achieve a delusive (they would say) sense of value and meaning to our lives (as we will see in Chapter 3). Nietzsche offered the utter self-justification of the Superman, which legitimated men like Hitler and Stalin in their own eyes. Karl Marx offered the sense, however delusory, of contributing to a workers' paradise none of us will live to see. Albert Camus offered the griping stubbornness of Sisyphus, refusing to knuckle under to an absurdly meaningless existence: "I haven't *quit!*" Choose your comforting illusion.

A major contributor to half-baked opinions is reductionism. We have an itch to simplify things to their least common denominator, which is perfectly natural. But it can be carried to the point of comforting falsity. Unfortunately, reality—especially the human reality—eludes our cookie-cutter definitions and theories. Humans are not merely rational animals, males are not all swagger and females merely yielding, love is not just physical and emotional. Too much that is pertinent is left out. Therefore, we will be speaking often about *polarities.*

Those who seek an understanding of God can take salutary lessons from searchers in the other disciplines. Scientists rely often on the principle of complementarity, one of the basic insights of quantum physics. In the twentieth century, scientists like Werner Heisenberg and Nils Bohr discovered some very disquieting but undeniable objective facts about the basic components of all matter. When you plunge down into the subatomic world, you can't expect the clear-cut, predictable activities you can legitimately presume in the everyday world that occasioned Newton's clockwork-universe physics.

For instance, in the commonplace world, you can fire a rocket from Cape Kennedy and predict it will impact Mars in a year or so, even if Mars is nowhere near that position at the moment. On the contrary, you cannot do that in invisible subatomic systems. They are not at all like the atomic model we're used to, with electrons whizzing in predictable orbits around a sun-like nucleus. That is no closer to the real picture than fifteenth-century navigators' maps are to a satellite photo. You can determine an electron's position *or* its velocity at any given time, but not both. The reason is that the means you use to determine the electron's location (bumping a bundle of energy off it) will automatically alter its speed and direction. Also, disconcertingly, at any given moment an electron may reveal itself acting like a pellet and an instant later like a wave. Which is it? Well, to put it simply, it's *both*—however unsettling that might be.

In 1932 Heisenberg won the Nobel Prize in Physics for the formulation of quantum physics, the most widely known principle of which is the uncertainty principle. At the core of the atom, in all that whizzing brew of matter and energy, the cause-effect predictability of big-world physics doesn't work so neatly. However, there is a *pattern* to those subatomic uncertainties, and those patterns reveal an order in the universe. We can't positively predict the outcome of individual molecular events, but thousands of like events fall into predictable statistical patterns. Just as we can predict the likelihood of divorce for children of divorce who drop out of high school and marry before age twenty, we can project what subatomic particles will do with fairly reliable accuracy. That's why quantum indeterminacy doesn't cause utter chaos.

The point of the principle of complementarity—another basic principle of quantum physics—is that if you hold *both* seemingly incompatible qualities (like solid and fluid electrons) to be true, you come to a much less simplistic and more adequate view of the situation. The principle is just a variant of what poets have long known as *paradox*:

- Sometimes you have to be cruel to be kind.

- Not to decide is to decide.
- Poetry is a way to say what can't be said.
- If you want the first place, take the last place.
- Unless you lose your life, you will never find it.

An embodiment of that polarity of opposites is the Taoist (Confucian) picture of the *yin* and *yang*, a circle bisected by a wavy line separating a black hemisphere from a white one, each with a small circle of the other color embedded in it. A synthesis of rest and movement, contrast and concord, an eternal interplay of opposites: masculine and feminine, movement and rest, suffering and serenity, immanent and transcendent, sacred and secular. All the contraries constitute an ever-vibrant, elegantly balanced but undulating synthesis. Any virtue, unbalanced by its polar opposite, runs amok into a vice: justice without mercy becomes vigilantism, love without common sense warps into possessiveness and enslavement, chastity without passion is barren. All realities reveal a dynamic interplay between polar forces, like the contrary poles of a magnet, which—when fused—create a force neither possesses alone. The lion lies down with the lamb without either one absorbing or diluting the other's unique qualities.

The same principle helps explain (a bit better) humans as both beasts and angels, scientific cosmology and Genesis, Teilhard de Chardin as scientist and saint. At first, the two elements seem as radically incompatible as fire and water. (But remember the one-time Native American word for whisky.) Rather than being the clear-cut dualism of René Descartes, the great mathematician and philosopher (1596–1650), who drew a rigid line between the knower *(res cogitans)* and the world *(res extensa)*, we have to become *involved* in the problem and walk around inside its apparent conflicts in order to understand them more fully, to "ride with" the truth. Mustangs and truth both rebel against secure bridles and corrals. They need not stone-faced judges but benign and impartial arbitrators. Complementarity is an organic, holistic attempt to harmonize contrary realities, both of which we know are somehow "there."

POSITIVISM

Descartes established a basic principle for any attempt to understand in any subject field: "In order to arrive at the knowledge of all things . . . never to accept anything as true unless I know from evidence that it is so." No reasonable person would object to that. But what would Descartes accept as reliable evidence? "Only that which presents itself so clearly and distinctly in my mind that I can have no occasion to doubt it."[2]

In Dickens's novel *Hard Times*, Thomas Gradgrind applies that exclusive rationalism to the education of the pupils in his company school:

> "Now what I want is Facts. Teach these boys and girls nothing but Facts. Facts alone are wanted in life. Plant nothing else, and root out everything else. You can only form the minds of reasoning animals upon Facts: nothing else will ever be of service to them. . . . Stick to Facts, sir!"[3]

No room in Mr. Gradgrind's school for fantasy, imagination, intuition, the unquantifiable, the "sense" of something larger than "Fact." In his school a horse is not a snorting steed with flaring eyes like Bucephalus; it is an equine quadruped. His students are not human spirits yearning for greatness, dreaming dreams, envisioning the unheard-of, exulting in the circus; they are reasoning animals, nothing more nor less. No sin in Gradgrind's school or world except sloth and lack of productivity. Nothing sacred except financial profit. There is *zero tolerance* of ambiguity, or hesitation, or doubt.

That mindset—which will yield to nothing but what *compels* assent—has reigned fiercely in every religious education class I've faced for forty-five years. "*Show* me! I'll believe if you can give me *scientific* proof." This from students who have never heard of Descartes except in some ill-defined way in geometry class. This persists despite the inescapable truth with which we began this chapter: we accept most of what we claim to be our own opinions without the slightest examination or hesitation, or that we operate our everyday lives on unfounded "certitudes":

- I'll be safe in the subway today.
- My doctor didn't graduate last in his class.
- I'm positive she won't tell.
- Of course I turned off the stove.
- This is clearly the career for me.
- We will truly love one another till death do us part.

As the Nobel Prize Committee recognized a century ago, we can *never* get that kind of inescapable Cartesian certitude, even in atomic physics. Natural science works extraordinarily well when it rigidly excludes the personal and subjective. ("Will this new discovery kill my thesis? If so, I simply have to start over.") Foreswearing any kinds of moral questions, about which pure science can make no legitimate judgments, researchers can build a quite dependable atomic bomb. A larger question, however, is whether the bomb should be used.

What is worse, to my mind, is that such uncompromising concern for certainty also infects some of the most devoted Catholics, who convince themselves they can offer that same unqualified assurance to those who contemplate accepting religion. They also confront those wondering if they might have committed themselves in their younger years to a set of beliefs that doesn't seem to hold up against what they've learned as adults. Well-meaning apologists for religion rarely realize their claim to inflexible confidence is actually an *obstacle* to others' acceptance. "You may be steadfastly convinced," they think, "but I just can't muster that. And until I can be as sure as you seem to be, I'll keep my options open, thank you." The apologists try, like well-meaning parents, to give the impression of having a fail-safe grasp of everything. But ingrained human finitude usually catches up with them and, as with Willy Loman, one serious flaw fissions *all* credibility.

I once received an e-mail from a nun who taught my book *Meeting the Living God*[4] for ten years with great satisfaction to her and her students, for whom it "clears the decks, plows the field, hooks the kids." However, a new priest assigned as chaplain took it to their diocese as heretical. He claimed (correctly) that its thesis is that we must accept less than absolute certitude on faith questions. However, he claimed (almost correctly), Vatican I declared unarguably such certitude is ready to hand. "If anyone says the one, true God, our Creator and Lord, cannot be known with certainty from the things that have been made, by the natural light of human reason: let him be *anathema*."[5]

The book does argue that with God questions—as with Heisenberg's physics—our fallible human minds must be content at first with a higher degree of probability that God exists than that God does not. Faith is neither submission to evidence that compels nor a blind leap in the dark. It is both: a *calculated risk*. In 1998 Pope John Paul II wrote that the soul is "fully free to give its assent" (*Fides et Ratio*, no. 67). But no one can be free *and* helpless to differ. Certitude, I believed, was the province of jihadists, Kamikazes, and high-school seniors.

Fresh from a seminary, this vigilant priest seemed to me, after forty-five years in the trenches, like a raw lieutenant fresh on the front, with no contact yet with the wily "enemy," criticizing methods of lifetime sergeants, and then running back to the War College for judgment from retired colonels with only theoretical recollection of wars fought on horses. They in turn would fire off orders to advance on Stalingrad, even though the oil in our tanks is black ice.

Further, the February 5, 2006, *New York Times* announced that one diocese had dismissed twenty-two staffers from its catechetical offices: "We have about 20,000 baptisms and about 20,000 marriages every year in this diocese, and the question we have to face is: Why are only a fraction of those people going to church?" A justified puzzlement, but the officials failed to see a difference between indoctrination and conversion, between catechetics, which explains the truths of Catholicism (theology), and apologetics, which tries to convince the listeners to accept them as meaningful (belief). Authorities' conviction that a statement is certain does not ensure its acceptance by the listener—

as if anyone sane and unbiased had no honest choice but to yield to it.

The *ne plus ultra* semantic arbitrator, the *Oxford English Dictionary,* defines *certain*:

> 1. Determined, fixed, settled; not variable or fluctuating; unfailing. 2. Sure, unerring, not liable to fail; to be depended upon; wholly trustworthy and reliable 3. Established as a truth or fact to be absolutely received, depended or relied upon; not to be doubted, disputed, called in question; etc.

However, the Thomists who forged that Vatican I *anathema* were flexible in their understanding of certitude! In the Thomistic mindset, certitude is a judgment not of any statement but of the degree of confidence within any believer. It does not exclude the possibility of error but only reasonable *fear* of error. More important, even the strictest Thomists allowed *degrees* of conviction, each of which they held as still validly "certain":

Absolute certitude is free of all *possibility* of error because the opposite would involve a contradiction—for example, the streets are bone dry; therefore, it is not raining. This restrictive meaning Descartes assigned to the word, as did the *Oxford English Dictionary.*

Physical certitude is free of all *probability* of error. The evidence excludes reasonable doubt (barring a miracle)—for example, a brick dropped out a window will go down; or all humans will die. This separates sane people from psychotics.

Moral certitude excludes all *reasonable fear* of error because the proposition depends on a consistent law of human behavior presumed operative without contrary evidence: The bus driver will not hijack us today; we vote on execution "beyond any *reasonable* doubt." Vatican I meant that absence of any substantive doubt is enough to qualify as "certainty."

Also, Cardinal Newman offers a source of surety called *informal inference.* Cumulative convergence of many small bits of experience generates dependable conclusions: "Why have I stayed with this woman fifty years? Well, uh . . . *everything*." But that is *experiential*; the speaker could not convince others of his conviction's truth, only of the degree of *his* certainty about it.

Moral certitude and Newman's informal inference seem exactly the "higher probability" *Meeting the Living God* offers skeptical students. Further, Vatican I affirms only that the existence of God *can* be known by reason; it is within the *capacity* of sufficiently trained minds. It does *not* claim unwavering faith will inevitably result if the individual only has good will.

TWO COMPLEMENTARY WAYS OF KNOWING

Whether logic is locked away in the left hemisphere of the brain and creativity in the right is a question in some dispute among neuroscientists. Some maintain the left brain is objective, rational, step-by-step logical, isolating focal issues from anything secondary, given to analysis (taking apart), working with definitions and formulas. On the contrary, the right brain is subjective, intuitive, sensitive to the influence of context, holistic, given to synthesis (seeing things whole), working with symbols and stories. Others dismiss that localized cranial distinction as wishful thinking. Whether that dichotomy of brain functions is objectively established or not, it has been a handy pair of "bins" to capture two quite different but undeniably real activities of the human knowing apparatus. I am not a body plus a brain. I am a person.

The eminent psychiatrist Carl Jung tried to do the same task with the terms *masculine* (dominating the material, rigorously excluding feeling or sentiment) and *feminine* (waiting to understand before leaping to conclusions, making allowances for specific situations), which were also somewhat unsatisfying because they seemed to those insensitive to nuance to identify elusive psychological qualities that denote *gender* (masculine/feminine) with the definitive physical differences of *sex* (male/female). Jung did not intend that at all. Clearly Hemingway and Robert Browning were virile males, but Hemingway's psyche was more "masculine" and Browning's more "feminine." The same difference, despite their identical sex, was true of Teresa of Avila and Thérèse of Lisieux.

Still another way of verbalizing the obvious truth of our differing ways of understanding is between the careful logic of the Greek or Western mind and the experiential judgment of the Hebrew or Eastern mind. To understand how the Western mind works, follow the careful steps in a Platonic dialogue or a question in the *Summa Theologica*, trace the meticulous architecture of the Newtonian universe or a Greek temple or an article in the *Oxford English Dictionary*. In contrast, submerge yourself in the puzzling koans of Hindu thought or the lush imagery of Keats or the imponderable mysteries of quantum physics. Both Eastern mysticism and modern physics require that the mind "rides with" the evidence as it moves rather than trying to lasso a whirlwind. We are handling realities that cannot be objectified, mastered, used—the way one might break and use a bronco. On the contrary, if we are humble enough, they capture us.

For the Greek mind, the impersonal trumps any personal involvement in the question; for the Hebrew mind, belief comes intuitively from personal *experience*. The Hebrew word meaning "know" is rooted in sexual union, as in "he knew his wife." Western minds find the conclusion to the Book of Job incomprehensible. God gives no satisfying *reason* to justify Job's unmerited agonies. Rather, Job abases himself before the *presence* of God and says,

> "I had heard of you by the hearing of the ear,
>   but now my eye sees you;
>   therefore I despise myself,
>   and repent in dust and ashes."
> (Jb 42:5–6, *NRSV*)

Before, he had known about God. Now he knew God.

Mr. Gradgrind was imperious in his attempts utterly to eradicate the human right-brain capacities, the feminine, the Hebrew. In a utilitarian, materialist, exclusively capitalist and scientific society, such an approach to understanding must be completely eradicated like heretics before the Inquisition or Jews from Hitler's Europe. Such certitudes are all rooted in precisely the same half-wittedness: stifled right brains. Even today in our more enlightened educational institutions, if there comes a budget choice between physics and choir, the option is moot.

Suppose, for instance, you are CEO of a major corporation with factories throughout the country. All plants are perking along except the major employer in Homeville, which, despite all efforts and management changes, is leaking red ink. What is the only strictly rational choice? Close it down and cut your losses. But the right-hemisphere, feminine, Hebrew mind asks unsettling yet very real questions. What about the workers? What about the tax base for the schools? What about auxiliary businesses, like service stations and laundromats?

Are we a charity?

Science and business and the law work much more efficiently if they leave aside such "peripheral," unsettling, bleeding-heart issues. Even psychology (as we shall see later) gets easier acceptance among skeptics as a hard science if it purposefully mistranslates Freud's carefully chosen term *die Seele* for the full person as "mind" instead of "soul." Easier that way to think of the offender as a brain, an object, a victim, rather than a subject responsible for poor choices.

Scholastic Aptitude Tests (SATs) are a reliable, left-brain index of a candidate's left-brain rational achievements, but any senior teacher will testify they are hardly the whole story—or even the most important element in predicting academic success (despite the wiles of prep providers and many parents' beliefs). Prudent colleges also ask for long-term class grades and teachers' recommendations—both of which are "tainted" by subjectivity. In that regard, as a test of a crime suspect's truthfulness, one might be wiser to credit his mother than a lie detector.

Pascal said, "The heart has reasons the reason does not know"—an equally tempting but inadequate effort to locate these two equally important, complementary powers: rational head, intuitive heart.[6] Jesus was definitely not a systematic theologian. He used not definitions and arguments but stories and metaphors that went not for the head but for the heart. It is almost impossible to conceive of someone finding proof for the existence and nature and personality of God at the end of a syllogism. God can prove himself only the way any other friend can: first, we notice God, then opening to time and talk, yielding trust when God seems ever-so distant and silent, and quite often echoing Jesus: "My God, my God! Why have you forsaken me?"

Friends don't prove themselves at the circus but by sharing a journey through hell.

THE VIRTUE OF DOUBT

Martin Heidegger tells us, "A faith that does not constantly expose itself to the possibility of unfaith is no faith at all but a mere convenience."[7] Disillusion and bull-headed doubt seem endemic to adolescence. But when one has reached sophisticated maturity, experience in the world *should* have brought any adult to evolved and solidified convictions and commitments. That could be true if an individual's wrestling with "the God questions" had kept pace with his or her grappling with the more insistent issues of earning a living, negotiating work relationships, coping with the self-disclosure and partnership of marriage, trying to understand kids, sensing old age and obsolescence coming nearer every year.

Anybody capable of coping with *Lord of the Flies* and trigonometry *ought* to feel doubt, smell rats, find flaws in the church. Why? Because they're *there*. Anyone with a mind broader than an unlettered peasant's *ought* to wonder if God might be a kindly hoax like Santa Claus. I don't *know* God exists; I'm *betting* God exists. I'm not absolutely certain Christianity is the best way to human fulfillment, but I'm more and more positive as I go on.

They are neither unconditional certitudes nor blind leaps but calculated risks.

Thus, it's disconcerting to have achieved a certain stability in life and suddenly start to ponder the "Big Life Questions," equipped only with convictions formed long, long ago by a quite different and much younger person, whose advice on any subject I'd be loath to accept readily today. I would hardly solicit the opinions of the person I was in high school on any serious issue now. If it's to be more than mere lifelong lip service, genuine religion is impossible except after a quest as harrowing as the adolescent and young-adult quest for personal identity.

There is no good hand-me-down religion. Internalized learning—even religious learning—has to begin with genuine curiosity, or it never begins at all. Authentic learning (as opposed to memorizing) is impossible unless learners question what they're told, poke holes, sniff for mildew, challenge the validity of all the shamans and all their shibboleths—till they can say, "This is not my parents' faith; this is *mine*."

However, most born-Christians are still taught that doubt and skepticism are temptations more lethal than lust. Adult Christians don't want to seem wavering in their faith for two reasons: one, their honest doubts could be contagious to those they love; and two, honest doubt might force them back to the considerable effort of reexamining convictions they thought were cast in bronze from their childhood.

A TOLERANCE FOR AMBIGUITY

> For nothing worthy proving can be proven,
> Nor yet disproven: wherefore thou be wise,
> cleave ever to the sunnier side of doubt.
> (Tennyson, "The Ancient Sage")

Making a case in law isn't the same as making a case in science, nor should it be true of theology, though too often it is. Advocates in court have a point to defend no matter what. The

judge has to make sure both "play fair." Developing such judicial impartiality rather than protecting vested interests was definitely not true in our religious training, even if we left that behind as recently as last year! There was a point to be defended,
no matter what.

Scientists believe in their theories beyond *reasonable* doubt.
Evolution is as assured as the spherical shape of the earth and the
molecular composition of matter. Scientists work from consequences to probable causes. So should seekers for human meaning. They corroborate their inferences with experience. So should
those who seek God. Modern biology has improved health care
and life expectancy. One would hope belief in God would produce a recognizable enrichment of human life. Jesus himself said,
"By their fruits you will know them" (Mt 7:16).

Francisco Ayala writes:

> Scientific explanations or hypotheses are creations of the
> mind, conjectures, imaginative exploits about the makeup
> and operations of the natural world. It is the imaginative
> preconception of what might be true in a particular case
> that guides observations and experiments designed to test
> whether the hypothesis is correct.[8]

Discoveries begin in the right brain: "What if we fiddled with
this bread mold? We could find a drug we can call penicillin."
Then that preconception moves into the left hemisphere to be
analyzed and tested. This is exactly what theologians have said
for centuries is their function: faith seeking understanding. "I
believe; help my unbelief!"

What if God-seekers were to go on their quest with the same
humility? Clues are not compelling, only suggestive. But when
they accumulate, they can point to patterns that offer a basis for
generalizations, predictions, and laws. They allow us to make
commitments without any reasonable doubt. The accumulated
personal experiences of prophets, mystics, and theologians are at
least analogous to the experiences of lab experimenters and theo-
reticians. Unbalanced religion can, indeed, spawn crusades and

witch hunts, just as unfettered science can breed Anthrax and Zyklon-B. But science can also produce aspirin; religion can produce Mother Teresa.

At the heart of every inquiry worth pursuit is mystery. Saint-Exupéry wrote, "The essential is always invisible." The most expert psychological work up, for instance, is no more a person than a plot summary is a performance. The Bohr model no more captures the atom than an old man on a throne embodies God. That elusive core within every reality led Einstein to say, "The most beautiful thing we can experience is the mysterious." Throughout our almost exclusively rational, left-brain schooling we worked in the unspoken belief that all questions are solvable. On the contrary, trying to encapsulate in words the profoundest truths in life—like love, courage, honesty, the human spirit itself—is like trying to pinch mercury. There are truths that don't (yet) fit snugly into our consolidating framework, which doesn't negate the whole—any more than quantum physics destroyed the usefulness of Newtonian physics in the everyday world or denying that snakes ever talked eviscerates the truth of Genesis. "There are more things in heaven and earth, Horatio, than are dreamt of in your philosophy." Or your science or your theology.

On one hand, no argument is knockout, compelling proof; on the other, no argument is wipe-out disproof: "There goes the whole house of cards." Gradual development of the eye doesn't contravene belief in an ultimate designer any more than the existence of an immaterial soul denies material evolution. If only we could speak (confidently) in theological investigations of "near conclusive" and "close to certain," we might have a chance of the same respectful hearing and suspended judgments that scientists receive in their classrooms and in the pages of popular news magazines.

The only alternative to making peace with mystery is the impoverishing choice to ignore it or the futile attempt to "solve" it. The wise Gilbert Keith Chesterton wrote:

Poetry is sane because it floats easily in an infinite sea; reason seeks to cross the infinite sea, and so make it finite. The result is mental exhaustion. . . . To accept everything is an exercise, to understand everything a strain. The poet only desires exaltation and expansion, a world to stretch himself in. The poet only asks to get his head into the heavens. It is the logician who seeks to get the heavens into his head. And it is his head that splits.[9]

When Mephistopheles made Faust his operatic offer for all unencumbered wisdom at the price of the scholar's soul, it was a worn-thin deal. Its first use in human history worked, too: "For God knows that when you eat of it your eyes will be opened, and you will be like God, knowing good and evil" (Gn 3:5, NRSV). To our great benefit, it failed to work later, out in the Judean wilderness: "All these I will give you, if you will fall down and worship me" (Mt 4:9).

The Tempter has always been shrewd enough to realize he wouldn't stand a tinker's chance offering "a very high degree of probability"! And as the Father of Lies, he has yet to discover the market value of forthright honesty.

These pages promise no more than a hypothesis worth exploring.

2

FUGITIVES FROM OURSELVES

Each person's psyche has an inborn evolutional
urge to grow, to integrate the contents
of the unconscious, to bring together all the
missing parts of the total individual into a
complete, whole, and conscious self.[1]
—ROBERT JOHNSON, WE

Each of us confronts the most profound pair of polarities—
between the deep need to "be somebody" and the equally intense
but contrary desire to "fit in." The tension usually begins in adolescence but too often is smothered by innumerable seemingly
more urgent pressures. On the one hand, we yearn for autonomy,
self-sufficiency, development of a unique identity rather than a
self defined by parentage, social standing, IQ, athletics, looks. On
the other, we crave community, sharing, belonging to, and draw-
ing fuller meaning from involvement with others and with the
world, the kind of companionship that sustained us since infancy
in the family.

The dichotomy poses itself in two different questions, both of
which invite us to find the *meaning* of life, some pattern in disparate elements of experience—order, significance, wholeness,
generating trust as a ground for confidence and hope.

Who am I? And how do I fit into all this?

Sadly (tragically) far too many answer the second question
first: How do I fit in? What do "you" want of me? What do I
have to do (wear, listen to, develop, change) to be accepted? Just

name it. *Anything*. But don't leave me out here alone, okay? Unfortunately, far too many—perhaps most—concentrate so intensely and exclusively on the second question that they never get to the first. The inertia we inherited from our simian cousins winces from the considerable effort to answer *any* questions, and our efficient Gradgrind schooling has much more important goals, like job qualification and the gross domestic product.

Abraham Maslow writes of an old psychology text he used as an undergraduate, "awful book, but it had a wonderful frontispiece."[2] The lower half was a picture of a line of babies, pink and brown and black, sweet, delightful, innocent, lovable. Above was a picture of a clump of passengers in a subway, glum, gray, sullen, sour. The caption said simply, "What happened?"

What, indeed?

The living death caused by such soulless conformism is celebrated in W. H. Auden's "The Unknown Citizen":

> (To JS/07 M 378
> This Marble Monument
> Is Erected by the State)
>
> He was found by the Bureau of Statistics to be
> One against whom there was no official
> 　　complaint,
> And all the reports on his conduct agree
> That, in the modern sense of an old-fashioned
> 　　word, he was a saint. . . .
> Was he free? Was he happy? The question is
> 　　absurd:
> Had anything been wrong, we should certainly have heard.[3]

Except for children whose lives are circumscribed and crippled by plains desolated in drought or by crack houses and the suzerainty of pimps, perhaps children's inborn sense of wonder lasts until the second grade, when life gets seriously focused on the deadening SATs. Before long we settle for a "realistic" acceptance of what seems unarguably "the way things are"; we adapt to the tedious and practical, which then becomes the norm, the distorted life we share with everybody else. We don't even notice how impoverished we are (but, somewhere in the depths of what might have been, we feel it).

This is not solely a problem of the mechanized modern world. Four hundred years ago Shakespeare's Macbeth bemoaned the same lifeless living:

> Tomorrow, and tomorrow, and tomorrow,
> Creeps in this petty pace from day to day
> To the last syllable of recorded time,
> And all our yesterdays have lighted fools
> The way to dusty death. Out, out, brief
>   candle!
> Life's but a walking shadow, a poor player
> That struts and frets his hour upon the stage
> And then is heard no more; it is a tale
> Told by an idiot, full of sound and fury,
> Signifying nothing.

What happens when human beings leave their souls—their self-definition—in the hands of others? What is the value of a human life in a directive society that itself has lost its soul? In Nazi German society and its wartime economy, manpower meant money. A prisoner in the Labor Office of the Dachau Camp kept a record showing just how valuable each of these "worthless" men and women was to the Third Reich (see Table 2–1).[4] Perhaps a paltry figure in itself, but multiplied by the fifteen million who died in the camps, it becomes a significant economic factor.

However, as we have seen, the truth is lurking "out there," despite a whole society's denial. If you treat gin like ginger ale, the truth will take its revenge. If you market sex like a seductive commodity, it will became no more special than sharing a gym session. And even if consumerist media convince easily persuaded citizens that the core of life is money, fame, sex, and power, something still struggling for humanity within the victims will rebel.

Figure 2–1. A Prisoner's Worth

Daily rental of prisoner	+ RM 6.00
Deduction for food	- RM .60
Deduction for use of clothes	- RM .10
Value of prisoner per day	+ RM 5.30
x Usual lifespan (270 days)	+ RM 1,431.00
Average proceeds from rational disposal of corpse (fillings, clothes, bones, valuables held by bursar)	+ RM 200.00
	+ RM 1,631.00
Cost of cremation	- RM 2.00
Total value of prisoner	+ RM 1,629.00
	($67.88 in 1998)

Perhaps in the insurgence of frustrated drive-by shooters, perhaps in the inexplicable suicides of suburban youth who had everything the consumerist society promised would make them happy. But at the very least it results in the dead-ended souls that Thoreau described 150 years ago: "Most men lead lives of quiet desperation."[5]

That thwarted humanity shrieks out in Paddy Chayevsky's razor-sharp satire *Network,* a 1976 movie, when the mad prophet, Howard Beal, the country's fourth-rated news anchor, finally loses all semblance of control on the air:

> "You've got to get *mad.* You've got to say, 'I'm a human being, goddammit! My life has *value*! So, I want you to get up now. I want you all of you to get up out of your chairs. I want you to get up right now and go to the window, and open it, and stick your head out and yell, 'I'm mad as *hell,* and I'm not going to *take* this anymore!'"

And all over the country, windows fly up, and millions of people who'd been sitting like brain-dead couch potatoes shout out: "'I'm mad as *hell*, and I'm not going to *take* this anymore!"

Then what? Back to their couches. And Monday morning, back in that subway. Then sitting at that same computer or assembly line or cash register.

What are they all missing?

One summer while I was writing at a lake cottage, every afternoon this big-bottomed, black Labrador retriever would amble up with a stick in her mouth and shoulder me out of repose to throw it into the lake for her. Well, I threw it, and she went gallumphing into the water after it. She'd return, hide behind a tree (so I couldn't see she'd dropped the stick to shake off the water). Then she'd sidle back, and we'd start it all over again until she was hacking and panting, and my arm was as limp as linguine. But she was still wagging that old tail like a hairy black metronome at top tempo. Whatever joy a black Lab can entertain, she entertained to the max. Even when she was exhausted. Why? Because she was doing what she was *born* to do: retrieve.

That's the question this chapter sets out to pursue: What will make us wag our tails with wild abandon, even when we're exhausted? What are human beings made for?

REDUCTIONIST HUMAN

There are some who assert that humans (and animals) are nothing more than highly complicated machines, products solely of heredity and environment, which can be manipulated by using the proper stimuli to effect a desired purpose—and the advertising industry shows a great deal of success in substantiating that view. One step higher, others assert that, despite the evidence, humans are merely more highly skilled and complex animals— and the daily papers suggest that many of our fellow humans try might and main to prove them right.

The absurdity (the obscenity) of the Dachau evaluation of a prisoner's worth should give the lie to such theoretical debasement of human beings to mere material entities. That same Nazi society published an anonymous assessment:

The human body contains a sufficient amount of fat to
make seven cakes of soap, enough iron to make a medium-
sized nail, a sufficient amount of phosphorus to make two
thousand match-heads, enough sulphur to rid oneself of
one's fleas.

Is that all Socrates and Shakespeare were worth? What is the
survival value of Bach?

Are humans merely somewhat complex bags of chemicals in
a controlling environment? I accept that a chair is not a rock-
solid entity but a swarm of particles moving so fast they *seem* at
rest. But is a horse really merely an equine quadruped? Is the
stirring I feel listening to "The 1812 Overture," with cannons
thundering over the Charles River, no more than a neurological
response to vibrations in the air?

Paradoxically, as brain study intensifies, some try to reduce
our soul functions to an interplay of body chemistry. In the
1960s, psychedelic drugs altered awareness through their effects
upon the brain; therefore, many equated the change in brain
chemistry with what others mislabeled an experience of God.
People high on marijuana may giggle uncontrollably—even
though there's nothing really funny happening outside their
heads. The cause is no more real than occasions when the unpleasantness of being tickled triggers the same giggles. Both the
drugs and tickling only agitate a nerve, not a person. It's the pre-
tense of having fun, the delusion of encountering God. But it
seems too reductionist by half to claim that such hollow results
from ersatz stimuli devalue what others call heartfelt humor and
an honest connection to God, each incited by an objective encounter with reality. Even more illegitimate to say it denies human distinctiveness completely.

One could say the same of the physical and emotional excite-
ment of a rock concert. The critical question is whether such
experiences have any permanent effect, whether they are true
spiritual nourishment or merely momentary stimulation of the
nerves. Saint Paul faced the same problem of discernment with
his charismatic Corinthians. "If I speak in the tongues of men and

of angels, but have not love, I am only a resounding gong or a clanging cymbal" (1 Cor 13:1).

Scientists will accept a cause as the proper source of an effect if it seems the simplest and most reasonable explanation (Ockham's Razor). At least for the moment, although others with more potent degrees than mine assert that I am merely a victim of my genes, chemistry, and the shifting vagaries of my environment, I stubbornly refuse to accept my freedom to choose as a cruel delusion. How can the courts punish criminals if "my electro-chemical circuitry made me do it"? If my sins are meaningless, then so am I. And all books are delusive waste paper.

But are we, as so many apostolically atheist scientists publishing today insist, better than mere mechanisms yet little more than apes with ever so slightly different DNA?

Many Australians believe it humane to cull rampant herds of kangaroos, not only because they savage crops but because the more numerous they become, the less food is available for the animals themselves and they face a greater likelihood of starving. But as Swift's "A Modest Proposal" points out, few would justify encouraging the Irish to overbreed so the English could feed on their children. The deaths of the villagers' children pose an objective limit to Dr. Frankenstein's freedom to pursue science unchecked. No matter what the society or what the proclamations of its pundits, there remains something objectively wrong about using your little sister as third base, about setting a live dog ablaze (as one could legitimately do to a Christmas pudding), about using human beings for experiments. The objective facts reveal that to anyone with open senses and an honest mind.

Early in the onset of Freudian psychology into American life, many intellectuals dismissed it as mumbo-jumbo, much as they brush aside New Age and Scientology today. At the time, ardent proponents of the great Austrian visionary were willing to mistranslate Freud's cautious word choices in order to have his insights more readily accepted as a hard science than some kind of bourgeois witchcraft.

In "Freud and the Soul" Bruno Bettelheim wrote: "Nearly all Freud's references to the soul and matters pertaining to the soul, have been excised in translation."[6] Where Freud speaks of *die Siele* (soul), translators have changed the word to "mind." Moreover *das Ich*, *das Es*, and *das Überich* become "Ego, Id, and Superego," whereas French translators render them *le moi, le ça, le surmoi*. To Freud's mind, the Ego is simply "the Me."

Freud chose words that are among the first used by every German child. Translating *das Es* (the It) into the Id and *das Ich* (the Me) into the Ego—into Latin rather than into English equivalents—rendered them cold and technical rather than associative. Introspective psychology was turned into behavioral psychology. Moreover, Ego becomes associated with pejorative meanings: egotistical, egoism, ego trip.

The most misleading mistranslation, mentioned above, is the use of "mind" where Freud used *die Seele*, "soul." Where he grapples with the workings of the psyche, he uses "soul" as the overarching entity that takes in all the other functions: Me, It, Over-Me, conscious, and unconscious. He is not talking merely of the mind, the intellect, but the whole *self*. Freud was a meticulous German stylist. If he had meant "mind," he would have written *Der Sinn*.

Coupled to a willingness to view humans as merely high-level animals, this simplification perverts Freud's direct and deeply personal appeals to our common humanity and makes them appear "abstract, depersonalized, highly theoretical, erudite and mechanized—in short, 'scholarly,'"[7] in order to achieve critical credibility in America.

No doubt at all that humans were late in arriving. The universe is 13.7 billion years old; earth is three to four—the first two billion or so taken up solely by single-celled organisms, incapable even of self-replicating. Homo sapiens is just a kid, merely about 200,000 years old. We deluded ourselves for thousands of years that we were the sole reason everything had happened. Then Copernicus and Galileo came along and, almost unforgivably, disabused us of our arrogant centrality. Nonetheless, despite the ardent reductionists, the evidence of human uniqueness is too manifold and intense to deny, even if the grounds for our objective superiority will never be established in a lab.

It is virtually undeniable that the human brain evolved through a process of chemical progressions in a developing universe. However, a sense of individual identity cannot root itself in matter alone. Our physical cells die off and are replaced, year after year. My body today is scarcely identifiable as the body I had at thirty. Yet I don't concomitantly slough off my *self*. Self-awareness is not merely sensitivity to neuronal explosions. We have firsthand experience of our selves and only bewildered acceptance of biologists' pronouncements about the comings and goings across our synapses and up and down our DNA.

The Theological Commission headed by Cardinal Ratzinger acknowledged in 2004 the likelihood of human physical evolution but saw the inherent contradiction of brute matter producing abstract thought—much less our conviction of a transcendent connection. In "Communion and Stewardship" it stated:

> Acting indirectly through causal chains operating from the beginning of cosmic history, God prepared the way for what Pope John Paul II has called "an ontological leap . . . the moment of transition to the spiritual." While science can study these causal chains, it falls to theology to locate this account of the special creation of the human soul within the overarching plan of the triune God to share the communion of trinitarian life with human persons created out of nothing in the image and likeness of God, and who, in his name and according to his plan, exercise a creative stewardship and sovereignty over the physical universe. (no. 70)

If we are no more than sophisticated chemical complexes or only higher-level apes, why hasn't the operating principle of the survival of the fittest bred out of us that frustration which wants to leap up and shout, "I'm mad as *hell*, and I'm not going to *take* this anymore!"?

The key is that, unlike any other nature, *human* nature isn't a command but an invitation. And utterly unlike the instincts programmed into other animals, an invitation can be refused.

POTENTIALLY HUMAN

No rock gets uppity and leaps to crack you on the back of the head, nor does it crumble into pebbles in despair. No carrot decides the soil is richer on the other side of the fence and uproots itself, nor does it refuse nourishment when it's available. No tiger we know of suffers pangs of conscience, nor can he resist copulation when he's in heat. But the daily papers give ample evidence humans can both degrade themselves and, more rarely, ennoble themselves.

Marble : acorn = cub : baby. At first glance, the marble and acorn seem alike. But there is a vast difference. Plant both, and the marble will just lie there inert; it hasn't the potential to be anything other than what it is. But the acorn has the potential to be vastly different from what it is: an enormous oak, unrecognizable from its tiny source. But that potential needn't be activated; the acorn can fall into swamp or onto concrete, where it will rot or shrivel. Similarly, a bear cub and an infant look and act quite alike; they spend their days eating, sleeping, excreting. Both will grow physically, but although the cub will never become more ursine, the baby has the capacity to become more profoundly human. The cub will definitely not become Smokey Bear, but the infant has the potential to become Leonardo da Vinci or Florence Nightingale. Or not.

If Cinderella is going to enjoy the ball, she has to make the effort to hollow out that pumpkin and overcome her disgust to gather six mice, one rat, and six lizards. And if she gripes about having to leave the ball at midnight, her fairy godmother can ask, "Honey, who said you could even *go* to the ball in the first place?"

The only limit to the evolution of the soul is death—and our own unwillingness to evolve our God-given capacities, a refusal that in itself is death-as-human.

Each of us was born a human being, but there is a whole spectrum of meanings to those words, ranging from pimps, pushers, and serial killers at one extreme (who are human, but scarcely over the line from brute beasts) all the way through ordinary folks to exemplars, the intimidating saints like Thomas More, Lincoln, Sojourner Truth, and Mother Teresa at the opposite extreme (who embody a humanity encroaching on transcendent goodness).

Since Aristotle, the definition of humans has been "rational animals," and it is an unquestioned promise of education that our school will produce a *mens sana in corpore sano*. We can, of course, arrive at some insight into ourselves by comparing ourselves with other animals. Biologically, anatomically, physiologically, there are countless resemblances. With rocks, we share mass, weight, electrical charge; like vegetables, we add the quantum-leap qualities of feeding, growing, reproducing; to that we add the further quantum-leap characteristics of other animals, feeling, movement, affection, awareness of brute facts like danger.

But the contrasts are even more remarkable. No question of our animality. The puzzlement is what we can do *despite* our animality. No tiger we know of gobbles a villager, then lumbers back into the jungle mumbling, "Oh, God, I've done it again. I need counseling!" As Abraham Heschel asks, "Would it be valid to define an ape as a human being *without* the faculty of reason and the skill of making tools?"[8]

No matter where else we want to localize it in our imagination, the reality within each of us that calls us to arise from our roots among lower levels of evolution to a dignity of which no other species is capable—what makes us *persons*—is the *soul*.

Those of us privileged to be present at a death can testify to a conviction of the reality of the soul. Even when the person has been in a coma, at the instant of death, a presence departs the room. No breath will fog a mirror; the EKG no longer pulses. There is nobody home there anymore. The life force, whatever it is that bonded all the disparate parts, is gone. That fact is beyond dispute.

THE HUMAN SOUL

Thus far in human history we've discovered no other species that is self-aware, open to the nuances of language, able to discern inherent meaning and value, capable of rational analysis and synthesis, able to imagine and create the not-yet-real, sensitive to right and wrong, able both to degrade and to transcend its beginnings. We are the only ones we know with the nature-specific hunger for answers, for survival beyond death, for purpose. If in fact, as atheists claim, there are no reasons, no immortality, no justification, then why are we the only species *cursed* by our very nature with hunger for food that doesn't exist? Again, why hasn't the law of survival of the fittest bred that frustration out of us? Throughout human history our stories have reflected journeys: Psyche, Odysseus, Aeneas, Abraham, Beowulf, Arthur, Don Quixote, Pilgrim, up to Frodo Baggins and Dorothy in *The Wizard of Oz*. We have the conviction (unless it is asphyxiated) that we are "going someplace," en route, and needful of a map (a myth) and an internal compass (a soul).

There are many words that cluster around the idea of the human soul: psyche, spirit, self, who-I-am, conscience, essence, character, life-force. I would like to use *soul,* as Freud did, to encompass *all* of those realities within each one of us. My soul—my real self—is what in me remains the same despite all changes and transformations I undergo. The soul is the sum of all the many-layered, complex forces within each of us that make us who we are, a scheme of values that gives a sense of rootedness to life, provides a center of gravity, a capacity not only for self-acceptance but also for self-transcendence.

Leo Rock describes human growth toward wholeness as clearing title to one's self.[9] An adult (distinguished from a grownup) is one who exercises exclusive ownership rights and responsibilities for his or her self. That self may be freely shared, but there is no question of either ownership or responsibility passing to someone else, not without total annihilation of the self in accepted slavery—to drugs, an ideologue, a boss, a turnkey, or more often perhaps, sheer apathy. Adults own and take responsibility for themselves. An adult is, therefore, in a word, self-possessed. For most of us the process of clearing title takes a lifetime.

Families try, without knowing really what they're about, to help a child become a person, and most often with little more than gut instinct to go on. When it comes down to it, most parents define their vocation as "giving them the best we can and protecting them from harm"—without ever sitting down and pondering what "the best" really means, except what everybody says is the best. What's more, unbalanced by common sense, those two loving goals can become corrosive to the child's soul, training the young person to expect life to deliver a bounty life simply can't deliver, an expectation that all the lights ought to turn green, a world where even inconvenience is crushing. One has only to look at overnight rock billionaires and airhead hotel heiresses, idolized the world over, but incapable of handling life as it is delivered.

We all want peace—just as we all want success, and the good life, and fulfillment. Trouble is, most of us never sit down and figure out just what peace and success and the good life and fulfillment really mean. Strange, isn't it? The whole purpose of human life—and nobody has time to figure out what it is. And God knows our schooling is too busy with such profound matters as finding the tangent of angle AOC and the law of supply and demand to help us find it. But one can't achieve a vague goal. Thus a lot of us feel a continual and indefinable malaise, like the hero in a Kafka story, because, by our very nature, we're sent on a quest. But we haven't the slightest idea what we're looking for.

There are so many states that orbit around the meaning of "a fulfilled soul" that we can consider only a few: happiness; wholeness; freedom; conscience; and animation of the potential soul, which is the human spirit.

HAPPINESS

As we will see more fully in the next chapter, all societies are looking for that Garden of Eden: the assurance of Mama, the workers' paradise, the American Dream, the kingdom, the womb, kindergarten, over Jordan, over the rainbow, heaven. It's the stuff of all vacation ads. But as the eminent psychologist William James wrote, "If merely feeling good could decide, drunkenness would be the supremely valid human experience."[10]

Our more thoughtful goal is not just to feel happy but to have a *reason* to be happy that doesn't evanesce with waking up or becoming sober. Happiness is not an emotional condition any more than genuine love is.

Freud said that within our souls there are two antagonistic polarities: *Eros*, the life wish, and *Thanatos*, the death wish. Eros yearns for challenge; Thanatos craves being unbothered.

It is Eros that impels us to risk marrying, committing ourselves to children we will not see for nine months, setting sail for "home" from Troy not knowing what the winds and waves portend, giving up something comfortable in the hope of something better.

Thanatos impels us back to the womb, closer to Eden than we will ever be again: warm, fed, floating, untroubled by doubts because we couldn't think. Eros will strive, even without attainment: In the going, I'm already there. Thanatos settles for the maximum return from the minimum input. The Eastern concept of Nirvana is fulfillment of Thanatos: liberation not only from all unpleasant sensation but from any sensation whatever, even from being an individual.

If Freud is right, the best in us does not crave the happiness, fulfillment, and peace of feeling good or being unbothered. The best in us craves the serenity of tightrope walkers, beat-walking cops, people who defuse bombs to save others, terminal cancer nurses: knowing we're doing the right thing and at least have a chance.

The Greek word for happiness is *eudaimonia*, "a good soul"; it means not *feeling* good but *being* good. It has nothing to do with emotions. Rather, it is a sense of being "at home" within oneself and within society and within the world. Self-possessed yet open to all. In that sense of *happiness,* victims at Auschwitz stumbling toward the gas chambers with their scrawny chins high and their souls in their own hands were happy. On the contrary, Hitler capering at Napoleon's Tomb over the humiliation of France was merely feeling good.

If the two capacities that differentiate us from other species are understanding and altruism, then the more broadly and profoundly we learn and love, the more often we will be surprised to find ourselves wagging our tails. As Viktor Frankl wrote, "Pleasure is, and must remain, a side-effect or a by-product, and is destroyed and spoiled to the degree to which it is made an end in itself."[11]

WHOLENESS

When Jesus said, "Be perfect as your heavenly Father is perfect" (Mt 5:48), he could not have meant *perfect* in its ordinary Greek usage: "unblemished, absolute, unconditioned." Only God can have those qualities. If, for instance, the church were perfect (as many wish), none of us could qualify. Rather, the Hebrew meant "whole," as a sphere is perfect, no matter how large, like the Confucian Tao. The fulfilled soul is an organic assembly of quite diversified parts, a unity captured more correctly in the terms "all together, wholehearted, wholesome."

The mature individual takes possession of the self out of the hands of memorized controls from parents (what Freud called the Superego: the Over-Me) and becomes his or her own father and mother. Like the good mother, he or she knows all misbehavior can be forgiven; like the good father, he or she knows what needs amending. The healthy soul not only senses the need to keep progressing but has at least a working grasp of where he or she wants to go. As Nietzsche wrote: "Whoever has a *why* to live for can bear almost any *how*."[12] We can stand incredible anguish if there is some felt context in which it makes *sense*. We will consider this more fully in the next chapter on myth.

FREEDOM

Despite being one of the most positive urges only humans share, freedom can be defined only in negatives, "unbounded, not coerced, uninhibited." And those who understand at what cost freedom is attained find true freedom unsettling and even terrifying—not only in others but in themselves, because we are born not truly free but with the *potential* for freedom. First, we are free—but always within the constraints of reality. The factual toxicity of cyanide intrudes on my freedom to gargle it; the law of gravity curtails my yearning to flap my arms and fly to the moon. I'm free to defy those limits but not their consequences. Second, we are not born free. We are born enchained to an Id we inherited from our beastly forebears, and we then gradually succumb to the shackles of a Superego of do's and don'ts from our elders and the media. Third, in accepting individual freedom, we yield to the truth that all other intelligent entities enjoy the same freedom—often with agendas on a crash course with our own. (And that includes the freedom of God.) Fourth, real freedom requires the possessor to think for himself or herself, to examine all the possible options in order to make a fully cognizant choice. And thinking takes an effort the Beast in us spurns. Fifth, choices exclude. I can stand before ten doors with absolutely no outside coercion and still be unable to bring my freedom into play, because to choose one automatically rejects the nine others, at least for now. I'm free to quit smoking the moment I surrender my freedom to light up.

There are surely far more reasons that freedom is not an unmixed blessing. No wonder Dostoevsky's Grand Inquisitor sneered at his captive, Jesus:

> "I tell you man has no more agonizing anxiety than to find someone to whom he can hand over, with all speed, the gift of freedom with which the unhappy creature is born."[13]

The opening paragraph of *The Spiritual Exercises of St. Ignatius Loyola* reads:

> The purpose of these Exercises is to help inquirers to take possession of the self, and to regulate their lives so their decisions will not be swayed by immoderate dependency. (translation mine)

This hearkens back to what we saw in the previous chapter about forming honest opinions. The essential first step is to see the objective facts as they reveal themselves, not as I wish they were or as "everyone" says they are. Then to judge them as *impartially* as I am able, not overly swayed by my own desires—*but not* (as some would argue) *without* including them; they are real and an integral part of the equation. At that point Ignatius suggests we put all the options on an altar in our imaginations, dust our hands of them, and walk away, leaving them in the hands of God. Then return later to ask what God's choice is.

Our greatest achievement is to set ourselves free of both the ferocious demands of the Id (and its support at every turn from the media) and of the imperious, unquestioned commandments of the Superego (from parents, teachers, peers, priests, government) by judging for ourselves what assertions are justified by the objective facts. That radical spiritual freedom is impregnable to theft, disaster, imprisonment. It faces down indigence, sickness, despair. It is impervious to pride, covetousness, lust, anger, gluttony, envy, and sloth. As Shakespeare wrote in Sonnet 94: "They are the lords and owners of their faces."

We must never lose a grasp on the ultimate freedom: the transformational value of *attitude*, not a habit of optimism vs. pessimism but a habit of hope rather than helplessness. Viktor Frankl writes that in the camps, "all the familiar goals of life are snatched away. What alone remains is 'the last of human freedoms'—the ability to choose one's attitude in a given set of circumstances."[14]

CONSCIENCE

If the primary purpose of basic schooling should be developing the skills to make honest decisions, the most important set of those opinions are what actions befit and ill-befit human beings. Like freedom, like humanity itself, only the *potential* for conscience is inborn. If it were otherwise, it would be impossible to explain Saddam Hussein or mob hitmen, who were born with the same capacities as Albert Schweitzer and Eliot Richardson.

Conscience is the ethical self, the person we truly are when no one else is watching. For some (again, perhaps for most) what they call "conscience" is really the jumbled bedlam within the Superego where all kinds of raucous voices shout contradictions at the self about honesty as the best policy and nice guys finishing last, about sex as surrendering and scoring, about yielding the first place and taking no crap. The purpose of adolescence and young adulthood, high school and college, *ought* to be eight to ten years when an individual forges his or her own self-validated set of moral guidelines—personally critiquing what "everybody says" against the objective facts.

But, of course, in great part American public schools, originally founded and funded to evolve citizens of informed integrity, are now forbidden to teach ethics because reductionists have convinced a majority that morality (which means no more than acting humanly) savors of an establishment of religion (which means a connection to a deity).

The natural law, the Confucian Tao, is a doctrine of objective values that holds that certain convictions are really true and others are really false, judged by what reality reveals to us of itself, no matter what my gut feeling says, no matter what my parents said, no matter what the church or the media or society or my wittiest teachers said. Laws, rules, and commandments are framed for people too self-centered or too lazy or too dumb to figure out for themselves that it is objectively wrong to savage your own children or spew raw sewage into a river.

The natures of things are of themselves laws, not in the sense of a societal law *(nomos)* but law in the sense of an inner truth *(logos)*. They are like the laws of mathematics or physics: a circle can never have four sides, and a square may not be round; water freezes at 32° F. (unless someone slipped in anti-freeze); it's undeniably wrong to use human beings like cattle; human sex is more than mere animal coupling.

THE HUMAN SPIRIT

If the soul is the human potential in each of us, the spirit is the soul ignited!

We find the full extent of what each human soul is invited to by focusing on those persons who have surged their way to the far end of the human spectrum, who have souls—or more precisely *are* souls—of unquestionable magnanimity: Buddha, Ruth, Hosea, Socrates, Jesus, Teresa of Avila, Dickens, Dostoevsky, Harriet Tubman, Gandhi, Annie Sullivan, Albert Einstein, Albert Camus, Cesar Chavez, Mother Hale. Some were not "holy" in a religious sense, but they all had a deep sensitivity to the needs and sufferings of humankind, extraordinary selflessness, loyalty to worthy ideals, and readiness to sacrifice even their lives for them.

More important, they seem to have had access to a serene dimension of reality that most people are too busy to discover and that the staunchest unbelievers scorn as wishful thinking, fit only for unlettered peasants and naive children. (Which is not *that* far off the mark.)

In great part, that deep-rooted sensitivity born in us is ever so slowly eradicated by the sensible, the practical, the efficient. Assaults on our sensitivities are commonplace—the scream of sirens, growling airplanes, brattling voices on cell phones, mind-numbing iPods, the world's children with harelips, bloated bellies, accusing eyes. To save our nerve ends from short-circuiting we withdraw behind scar tissue, as Eliot said, "living, and partly living."

Gerard Manley Hopkins's "God's Grandeur" sums up the tragic human loss, like hungry Esau pacifying his insistent hunger for a bowl of stew at the cost of his birthright:

> The world is charged with the grandeur of
>   God.
> It will flame out, like shining from shook foil;
> It gathers to a greatness, like the ooze of oil
> Crushed. Why do men then now not reck his
>   rod?
>
> Generations have trod, have trod, have trod;
> And all is seared with trade; bleared, smeared
>   with toil;
> And wears man's smudge and shares man's
>   smell: the soil
> Is bare now, nor can foot feel, being shod.
>
> And for all this, nature is never spent;
> There lives the dearest freshness deep down
>   things;
> And though the last lights off the black West
>   went
> Oh, morning, at the brown brink eastward,
>   springs—
> Because the Holy Ghost over the bent
> World broods with warm breast and with ah!
>   bright wings.

However, humanity isn't that easily foresworn. The Holy Ghost is not that readily dismissed. At times we are caught by surprise, "off guard," by the carouse of summer stars, the rhythm of the rain, the harrumph of the waves, holding a newborn infant, hearing "I love you, too." Athletes feel it sometimes, losing the self in the game yet never being more a self. We sense it escaping from an accident, hearing the call to stand down, knowing "she's going to pull through." They are, even for unbelievers, the "Oh, my God" moments. As surprising and unpredictable as a rainbow.

In those numinous moments we feel suspended in an "eternal present," a sense that there is more to life than we've settled for. We can't force them to happen, only be open to them. And, unlike the momentary highs from LSD or mescaline, we don't feel "let down" after.

William James writes:

> It is as if there were in the human consciousness a sense of a reality, a feeling of objective presence, a perception of what we may call "something there," more deep and more general than any of the special and particular senses.[15]

And James quotes the poet James Russell Lowell, who put it more accessibly:

> I remember the night, and almost the very spot on the hilltop, where my soul opened out, as it were, into the Infinite, and there was a rushing together of the two worlds, the inner and the outer. . . . I could not any more have doubted that HE was there than that I was. Indeed, I felt myself to be, if possible, the less real of the two.[16]

God is astonishingly polite. He will knock on our doors at times but never presumes to enter uninvited. We know beyond logic when we have made the connection to the beyond (which is the root meaning of "religion"), when we sense we exist in a dimension of reality unimaginably broader and more profound than the world's self-centered concerns, when we can surrender amicably to a Power greater than ourselves with a sense of freedom and elation. The very core of our soul responds with a heartfelt "yes!" And the test of the conversion after that is our everyday open-mindedness, openheartedness, openhandedness.

Before that, we careen from hither to yon in the pursuit of happiness, without ever asking before we set out on the quest just what happiness means, what will make us wag our tails, even when we're exhausted. And all the time we've been like Helen Keller, bewildered and thrashing about aimlessly in the sunlight.

3

FEELING "AT HOME"

Things fall apart; the centre cannot hold;
Mere anarchy is loosed upon the world,
The blood-dimmed tide is loosed, and everywhere
The ceremony of innocence is drowned;
The best lack all conviction, while the worst
Are full of passionate intensity. . . .
And what rough beast, its hour come round at last
Slouches towards Bethlehem to be born?
—WILLIAM BUTLER YEATS, "THE SECOND COMING"

When a child wakes up from a bad dream and finds herself alone in the dark, reality is all askew; she's lost in a landscape with no reassuring landmarks. So she cries out in terror, and her mother's there, turning on the light, rocking the child in her arms: "It's okay, honey. Everything's okay." At that moment the mother is the high priestess of meaning. Wordlessly, the child feels harmony restored to her world: things are as they should be. She is once again "at home" in her world. All of us, no matter what our age, need some reassurance that "it's okay, honey."

In the womb and for the first years after birth, infants always felt "at one" with the mother. But now, when the mother goes back to work within a few months or weeks, the child feels disconnected, a deep unfilled need for continuous contact with one sensorily identifiable human being throughout the first two years of life. Going back to work is, in many cases, a wrenching choice but a matter of sheer survival. A question could arise, though, when the mother's income is "essential" only to keep up a certain standard of living. But what do those words mean? Is lifestyle happiness? Is a child's disorientation worth it?

Yet in our present ethos, even among those with some tentative religious ties, even among the highly prosperous and well degreed, even among the formerly idealistic young—especially the urban young—life too often seems at odds with us: one damn thing after another; "The centre cannot hold"; "What's it all about, Alfie?"; "Is this all there is?" By our very human nature, we're in ardent quest for success, fulfillment, happiness. But if someone asked, "Where are you off to," many would have to shout back, "Don't ask me! Ask my *ho-o-o-rse!*"

This is true of most "advanced" societies today. Once, we were at one with nature, the soil, plants, animals. When that connection atrophies, as a people we feel disconnected. We see this in the history of Native Americans, dragged into "civilization" and finding themselves lost, aimless, and disenchanted. Bereft of a centuries-old matrix of meaning, they suffered a pervasive sense of rootlessness, wandering, aloneness. One need only cruise the tables at Vegas or rove the malls and watch all the dead eyes bespeaking haphazard lives.

Home is a sacred place, even for the nonreligious. Just as religious people believe that, at the church doorsill, they step from secular into sacred space, all of us believe there is a special space beyond our own doorsills that simply ought not be violated. This is my place, where I can close the door on chaos and find some kind of cosmos, peace, belonging. "Home is," as Robert Frost said in "The Death of the Hired Man," "the place where, when you have to go there, they have to take you in." Objects in that home are also "holy": a box of letters, an old photograph album, mementos on a desk that say, "This is mine; here I belong."

Christmas is a sacred time even for those without religion: a time to go home, to recapture a meaningful past where family made everything more or less make sense. Thanksgiving and Christmas are the busiest times for airlines. But without family, Christmas can be the most soul-harrowing time of the year. Christmas is also the busiest time for suicides—who die of homesickness. We remember. And we want to go back when things were right.

There are three basic human drives: to pleasure, to power, and to meaning. Our present society offers us ample (often spurious) means to achieve the first and second, but little if any help in achieving meaning or wholeness. We still feel haunted by nostalgia for the rightness we sensed before separation from our mother.

But home is also the place we must leave. In folktales, the stories societies have told for thousands of years to explain growing up, the heroine or hero is forced to leave home on a perilous journey or some displacement (like a wicked stepmother) has made home not the same source of reassurance it had always been. You find this story in the great myths and parables: the *Odyssey* and the *Aeneid,* the uprooting of Adam and Eve, Abraham and Sarah, Noah, Rachel, the missions of Buddha, Jesus, Paul, and Mohammed, *The Divine Comedy, Pilgrim's Progress.*

The tale of Hansel and Gretel, for instance, says children sooner or later must leave the nest and discover how to make their own way with their wits. And that is also true of the great folktales of our own day, as we will see. They mirror the polar tension each of us feels in our soul (not mind or body) between wanting to belong yet wanting to become an independent self.

But even if the journey lies away from home, the goal is always to return home. As Dorothy says when she clicks her red slippers, "There's *no* place like home." But she returns not as the dismissible girl she was when she left; she is now becoming a woman. The goal of the evolving soul is to bring cosmos out of chaos again, but it will not be the old order but a new, different, richer one.

MYTHS: SYMBOLIC STORIES

The first step toward a meaningful life story is affirming the world *as it is*—good and bad, darkness and light—rather than hoping it will yield to our expectations. Every natural human impulse—sexuality, aggression, sensitivity, doubt—must not be denied or subjugated or suppressed but sublimated, integrated, made fruitful. As Dag Hammarskjöld said, "For all that has been—Thanks. For all that shall be—Yes."[1] The only alternative is neurosis. We must forgive the past and face the future with serenity and confidence. But for that we need a map. Without one, we are as adrift as Updike's Rabbit Angstrom or Kerouac's Dharma Bums. It may be a chart as primitive as a Renaissance sea captain's, but we can constantly update it. That's what a personal philosophy of life—a myth—is for.

The word *myth* has two valid but contradictory meanings, as different as *false* and *true*. Its more common usage means a widely held delusion, as in "Vietnam dispelled the *myth* that America could never lose a war." The other, opposite meaning is a story that acts like a symbol, trying to capture a truth of human life in a right-brain, metaphorical way rather than in a left-brain, philosophical way—as in the *myths* of the awakening Buddha, Sisyphus, the Grail. These stories have been retold for thousands of years, passing from one culture to another so often that the details which individuate them to a particular culture erode and what is left is a scheme embodying a *universal* truth, applicable to any human being of whatever time or culture.

Do I matter? Am I useful? Have I value? We need some context against which to justify the struggle and assuage our fear of futility. We need a *pattern* to the disparate elements of our experience, so our very being is not haphazard. We need to feel our selves and our toil have significance. (The activity of a beehive or assembly line may be purposeful, but it's not meaningful.) Without a felt sense of purpose, life "is a tale told by an idiot, full of sound and fury, signifying nothing."

Meaning, purpose, commitment are inseparable. Without them, we have no hope of fulfillment. For those who always keep their options open, life is merely something that happens to them.

Symbols

Rational definitions are essential if we are to understand the world and ourselves, but they simply can't go far enough when we try to understand realities peculiar to human beings. A dictionary can box in any reality from aardvark to zymurgy, but in no case does it help us grasp anything's meaning, especially the prickly realities specifically human: love, hope, pride, integrity, trust—even meaning itself. For that, we need symbols. My dictionary takes forty tightly printed lines to define *love,* and when I come to the end of them, I'm still befuddled. But a little girl with meticulously corn-rowed hair "says" love, too, and a great deal more satisfyingly than Noah Webster can.

A symbol is an inadequate way to make physical a reality that actually exists but is not physical: death (skull), achievement (diploma), freedom (wings). A symbol, then, is like the clothes the Invisible Man had to don in order to be seen. The symbol is inadequate because it is only an approximation, not an experience of the actual reality, but rather like describing green to a blind person as "chewing mint leaves and sucking the juice." Not the reality, but at least a bit better than nothing. Problems arise from taking the symbol literally, thus either making it into an idol (fundamentalism) or poo-poohing it as childish (rationalism).

Some symbols are universal, exuding the same connotations no matter what the time or culture: natural symbols. Other symbols have meaning only within the framework of a particular time and society: culturally conditioned symbols.

Fire, for instance, is a natural symbol of energy, zeal, enthusiasm. Unchecked, it is rapacious; harnessed, it gives power. From ancient Druid pyres to modern beach bonfires, fire focuses those assembled, a challenge to the darkness. Thus, any person, in any culture, can resonate to the connotations of the fiery Phoenix resurrecting from its own ashes.

Other symbols are culture bound, and in order for them to be revelatory, one has to be "in on" the symbol matrix of a people. A pinch of incense on coals at the foot of an emperor's statue is a trivial act—except when some believe the emperor divine. An American flag is just a piece of cloth, but it's foolhardy to burn it at a construction site. A name on a document is simply a configuration of ink, but it takes on a different meaning when one reads "I do so swear" above it. Then that pictograph is the physical manifestation of my name, my word; it puts my *self* on the line.

In some symbolic stories, like Shakespeare's, the culturally conditioned classical symbols are so thicketed we need footnotes. But most myths have passed through centuries from culture to culture, so most culture-bound symbols rubbed off or changed to some reality more universally understandable. And these stories were composed for simple people. Still, they do take some pondering. Some are surprised, for instance, to learn that the three little pigs are really one pig who finally learned his lesson, and when he boils the wolf (the Id), rather than burying it, he eats it. He is assimilating and sublimating Id power rather than repressing it.

You can't be in a literalist frame of mind when you read folktales and myths. Why did Jack risk going up the beanstalk the third time when the golden goose he'd picked up on his second trip guaranteed him lifetime solvency? (Because money isn't enough in human life; Jack needed the enrichment of his "feminine" soul, that is, the music of the golden harp who was an enchanted princess.) Why did Hansel trick the witch with a bone and Gretel with an oven? (The Freudian symbolism obviates explanation.) Why would Little Red Riding Hood be dumb enough to get into bed with a wolf, who looked no more like her grandmother, even in a nightcap, than Lassie? (Because girls Little Red's age have gotten into bed with "wolves" for centuries and regretted it.)

Archetypes

Cro-Magnons thirty thousand years ago had the same bodies we do today, which put the same demands on those primitives as they do on us: food, sleep, health, warmth, shelter. Everywhere and always the primary human concern is to stay alive. But food, clothing, and shelter are not enough. We also live by being related to what is beyond the limits of our own skins—parents, siblings, neighbors, the environment, the mysterious Beyond-the-Beyond—

none of which can be captured in definitions but only in evocative symbols.

What's more, those earliest humans went through the same predictable but challenging physical and psychological stages as we do today: birth, infancy, childhood, learning the skills to survive and the customs of the tribe, puberty, parenthood, aging, and death. And the people of every culture between Cro-Magnons and people today have had the same human bodies and the same stages of human growth: Egyptians, Aztecs, Polynesians, Zulus, Iroquois. Whether we lived in a cave in southern France or live in an apartment in Chicago, no matter how brutal or sophisticated our surroundings, we still have the same bodies, the same stages of human growth, the same challenges to find a reason to keep going.

Therefore, we respond to the same stories human beings for thirty centuries have found helpful to understand those physical and psychological changes. Jung called these "archetypes," universal ideas grounded in changes of the human body and soul. Despite differences in hairiness, posture, food, weapons, shelters, every human story is the same story from birth to death. As Joseph Campbell says, it's the same play but translated into different languages by different players. The story hasn't changed since the first *Homines sapientes* lifted themselves off their knuckles, looked around at the world, and asked, "Why?" And if we are amnesiac about history, we can only improvise. Then we die.

Very often at the outset of the story the hero or heroine is lost, or summoned, or sent away. He or she embarks on a journey, encountering helpful folk or animals as well as disconcerting dragons, griffins, orcs, and other unpleasantnesses, and in such uninviting locales as fire pits, sealed rooms filling up with water, spacecrafts without propulsion but plenty of suspicious creaks and alien grunts. If the hero or heroine doesn't actually descend into the underworld (and often that does happen), he or she at least contends with fearsome approximations of it.

The ages have discovered, again and again, that the only place one takes ownership of one's soul is on a journey through hell.

Concentration camp survivors will validate that. We think we know ourselves, possess ourselves, until we plunge to rock bottom. Then, as with King Lear, our eyes are truly opened.

The Wizard of Oz

The story of that journey to selfhood is portrayed from a girl's perspective in the ever-popular *The Wizard of Oz,* which was published in 1900 and was made into a movie in 1939, at the end of the Great Depression, when Europe was already at war and America was teetering on the brink of it. It came at a time when people needed to see in recognizable images the clash of good and evil, a need for hope—and friends—in the midst of despair. Hollywood has always been able to reflect America's daydreams, and a myth is for a society what a dream is for an individual: a way of symbolically explaining what troubles us.

Most of "The Wizard of Oz" is, in fact, a dream, and like all dreams it contains the residue of Dorothy's day before the cyclone hit: Miss Gulch, who has taken Toto, reappears as the Wicked Witch; the three farmhands as the Tin Man, the Lion, and the Scarecrow; and Professor Marvel as the Wizard.

The story is a myth of a young girl forced (by the cyclone) to leave home and go out on her own, and it deals with the two questions that have bedeviled every adolescent for the last thirty thousand years: Who am I? and Where do I fit in? Before, Dorothy had moped around the farm, getting in everybody's way, dreaming of an ideal world somewhere "over the rainbow." She's an orphan (no explanation why), and the strongest figure in her life is Auntie Em, a no-nonsense, hardworking lady. Most of the males in the black-and-white story that bookends the dream are nice but ineffectual: Uncle Henry, the three farmhands, Professor Marvel. In order to be a woman, does Dorothy have to be like Auntie Em?

Then, as the technicolor dream begins and Dorothy finds herself "over the rainbow" in Munchkin Land, she's immediately hailed as a heroine for inadvertently killing a wicked witch. As a reward, Glinda the Good Witch gives her the dead witch's red slippers. But why doesn't Glinda send her back to Kansas right away? The "power" is in the slippers, and she already has them. But Dorothy has to find her power for herself, in herself.

On her way, she falls in with three friends, who—just as Toto is a symbol for Dorothy's own frisky spunk—are symbols of her own lack of self-esteem based on not being intelligent enough, loving enough, courageous enough. During their many adventures, it becomes clear that however beautiful Oz might be, it is mostly like this world. The difference is that in this dream world it is very clear where good and evil are; they are not, as in this world, all deceptively smeared together.

It is Toto (Dorothy's curiosity and pluck) who causes her to throw water on the witch when she is trying to burn the dog and who unmasks the Wizard. Unlike the roaring projection who terrified the foursome, he is just a fussy old man manipulating levers. But he is quite unlike the wicked witches. "Oh," says Dorothy, "you're a very bad man!" But the Wizard answers, "Oh, no, my dear. I'm a very good man. I'm just a very bad wizard."

The answer is not wizardry but kindness and wits. By the time they arrive back at Emerald City with the witch's broomstick, the friends have proven that they had more than enough heart and brain and courage all along; all they lacked was belief in themselves. So the Wizard merely makes it official by giving them symbols that capture those inner realities: a heart-shaped watch, a diploma, a medal. And the Wizard promises to take Dorothy back to Kansas in a big bag of hot air. But it's not a man, however wise or kind, who can get Dorothy home. It is Glinda the Good who tells her she must get back to Kansas by clicking her red heels and saying three times, "There's no place like home."

The magic in the slippers is Dorothy.

When she returns—just as Psyche and Odysseus on their return from the underworld—she is changed. She has brought home a self she can be proud of—a soul energized by her adventures.

Star Wars

The same journey to evolve a soul is told in the *Star Wars* films. In discussing them, Joseph Campbell told Bill Moyers the

success of the films was not merely the exciting production values, but that they posed for people who needed it (especially the
young) an uncluttered, unsanitized image of the clash between
good and evil. "They needed to be reminded of idealism, to see
a romance based upon selflessness rather than selfishness."[2]

The fact that the evil power was nameless (only the Empire)
allowed it to stand for any monstrous, heartless, totally rational-
istic force in the modern world. When Darth Vader's mask is
removed, we see an unformed man who has never developed a
soul, as unaccountable as the faceless generals who sent William
Calley into My Lai, or the godfathers who order mass slaughter
during their grandchildren's baptisms, or terrorists who approve
booby-trapping school busses and later receive the Nobel Peace
Prize: men who have bypassed their own souls.

When Moyers asked his son why he saw "Star Wars" so often, he replied, "The same reason you read the Bible all the
time."

Quick-Fix Myths

As typical myths show, the gods emancipate our souls only at
the price of considerable effort. But in a time when, as Carrie
Fisher says in the 1990 movie *Postcards from the Edge,* "instant
gratification takes too long," we are bamboozled into thinking
one weekend given this or that placebo drill will set our whole
lives to rights.

Sam Keen catalogues these quick-fix myths:

In the milieu of what has been variously called "the New
Age movement" or humanistic psychology, I found an
uncorseted spirituality that abandoned the classical effort to
open a path between faith and reason that had been so
important to me. No one in the Age of Aquarius seemed
concerned to offer reasons for what they believed, much
less to gather evidence to support their conclusions. The
New Age was credulity gone wild—belief in healing crys-
tals, channeling of entities, out-of-body experiences, pyra-
mid power, sorcery and prosperity for all, and you can tune

your Body, Mind, and Spirit to the Universe with the fabulous Cosmic OM Tuning Fork ($34.95 plus shipping and handling).[3]

With a smug, gnostic certitude that would embarrass even a televangelist, unsubstantiated "authorities" offer universal blueprints and suppress all contrary opinions or even honest questioning. At their most pernicious, you have Jim Jones of Jonestown and David Koresh of Waco. At their best, they seem merely silly. But as P. T. Barnum opined, "There's a sucker born every minute."

Perhaps one acid test of any philosophy (or religion) is whether its adherents can laugh at themselves—and even at the ways they sincerely express their beliefs. But certainly the fundamental criterion is whether any world view generally and genuinely produces believers who are more openhearted, more openminded, more openhanded than any nebbish off the street.

LEAVING HOME TO FIND HOME

The same basic journey themes appear in the myths of Egypt and Greece, in Buddhism, Judaism, Christianity, Islam, Native American religions, the Arthurian legends, and all the myth systems the world over since the rise of human beings on this planet. At the bottom of the dark abyss (hell, underworld, forest, Mount Doom, the depths of the sea) is the light of salvation (one's hard-won soul, meaning, purpose, justification). It is only at the bleakest moment that transformation to adulthood—conversion—comes.

There must be some reason for the basic similarity despite the different symbols chosen. The key is that myths are clues to the spiritual potentialities of human life, no matter in what time or what culture. They serve not so much to give an understanding of life as to embody the *experience* of being truly, humanly alive. They give inner sustenance in crises, making them bearable. They give models of endurance, like Harry Potter and Princess Leia.

Stories of the call to leave home on a quest are so constant in every culture that such a call must be a universal in human spiritual growth. The hero or heroine is one who gives his or her life to a struggle bigger than the individual's own interests and is ennobled by it. The journey is always a "death" and rebirth; it is embodied in the heroic act of a mother's labor and giving birth, risking her own life that a new life might emerge. The Chinese *Tao Te Ching* says the same: "When you have been hollowed out, you will be full." A crucifix says it too.

The most desolating place a human can inhabit—hell on earth—is an utter sense of emptiness when one's sense of belonging, one's confidence in a firm context, evanesces. That is the soul-searing experience of ultimate despair: "Mommy's gone away, and she's never coming back."

The purpose of human life is the quest to find a soul, a self, an internal compass. We've known that for thirty thousand years now. And our libraries are filled with the maps of those who have quested before. But does anyone know a school that helps the young find and begin to own their souls? Are Glinda and Obiwan Kenobi beyond recall? Are we Christians bent only on saving souls from some future hell, or from atrophy here and now?

4

SCRIPTURE AND MYTH

*Because Scripture is inspired and presumably this
inspiration was for the good of all, there has arisen
the fallacy that everyone should be able to pick up
the Bible and read it profitably. If this implies that
everyone should be able to find out what the
sacred author is saying without preparation or
study, it really demands of God in each instance a
miraculous dispensation from the limitations
imposed by differences of time and circumstance.*[1]
—The Jerome Biblical Commentary

"I'm digging my own grave with my mouth." Literalists—
whether skeptical literalists or naive literalists—will read that
claim and come away baffled. How long would it take this man
to dig a hole six-feet-by-six-feet-by-two-feet with his mouth?
Literalists not only miss a lot, but they're resolutely humorless.

Every day, without even thinking, we use figurative language
and instantly translate it into perfectly comprehensible communication: "I'm gonna kill you, Junior"; "pea brain"; "motor
mouth"; and on and on. Nonliteral language is a perfectly valid
way to communicate ideas—even though it's parabolic, around
the corner. But a great many people—whether distrustful or
credulous—refuse to allow the Bible to use the same kind of ver-
bal "roundaboutness."

Not-yet-convinced Christians are harmed by well-meaning
instructors who leave them with the false impression that the
Bible is nothing but a bunch of stories. Such teachers don't seem

to have realized—or been able to convey—that neither Aesop nor his audience believed turtles and rabbits at one time made wagers on a race, but they saw within the story a real truth: slow and steady wins the race. This is the sense in which some scripture is myth: stories trying to embody truths. A great deal of scripture does put forth otherwise verifiable facts: the gradual origin of the earth, the Hebrew slavery in Egypt and Babylon, the life and death of Jesus, the progress of the early church. But a great deal is also trying to mediate supra-historical truth: the undeniable moral weakness of humans, the seductive emptiness of earthly pleasures, the reciprocal relationship between God and humanity, the only temporary negation of death. The author of Genesis, writing about the same time as Aesop, did not expect his audience to believe that snakes once talked to nude women in the park, but he was trying to capture a very real truth: only human beings go against God's will for them.

Similarly, all our pictures of God are false in the literal sense; God exists outside material reality and thus has no chin for a beard, no right hand, no genitals. The real God is never brought to tears nor does God erupt in wrath. If heaven and hell are outside time and space, too, where did they harvest the pearls for those pearly gates, or mine all the coal for a hell that has raged at least since the rise of *Homo sapiens*? The problem is not with the reality of heaven or hell but with the inadequacy of our symbols. We could just as easily see the reality of heaven as a beautiful place in the mountains (as C. S. Lewis does in *The Great Divorce*) and hell as an inescapable hotel room inhabited by three people who detest one another (as Sartre does in *No Exit*).

Surely a huge feathery personage swooping into Our Lady's kitchen in Nazareth (as angels do in paintings) would have scared the wits out of her. And if the sky around Bethlehem were literally filled with blazing beings belting out their (nonexistent) lungs like the Mormon Tabernacle Choir, someone in the area besides the shepherds must have noticed. At the empty tomb in Mark's version of the gospel, the women are greeted by a young man wrapped in a white cloth; in Luke, it is two young men in white; in Matthew, it is an angel; in John, two angels. Which was it? It makes no difference! All four are saying precisely the same thing, with different symbols. Young men wrapped in white—or angels—were never literally true in the whole Bible; rather, they are symbols for the real but invisible presence of God. Luke and John, knowing that the Law required two witnesses for validity, simply doubled the number of witnesses.

Extreme literalists find a great many more problems in the scriptures than they need to, and surely more than the original writers intended or than the original readers felt. Skeptical literalists (rationalists) take one look at the Tower of Babel, the star of Bethlehem, Peter and Jesus walking on water and—taking them as if they actually happened—scoff them away as myths in the self-delusional sense. Credulous literalists (fundamentalists) blithely accept the talking snake, the mass suicide of the Gadarene swine, the multiplication of the loaves and fishes as if they had the same rock-solid verifiability as the assassination of John Kennedy. Thus they have to keep everything religious in one hemisphere of the brain, walled off from everything they know from paleontology, psychology, and physics in the other. Literalists, of either persuasion, miss out on a lot in the Bible. Jokes, too.

Stories can tell very real and important truths about human life without having literally, historically occurred. Aesop's fables tell us—symbolically rather than literally—that it is one thing to propose belling the cat and quite another to execute the proposal. Folktales have done the same for centuries: "Cinderella" tells the same truth as our Lady's Magnificat, that the lowly will be raised up; "Beauty and the Beast" says anything ugly, once it is loved, becomes beautiful; "Jack and the Beanstalk" shows (rather than tells) that every young man, from slingshot David to today's climbing executive, will have to fight the big boys if he wants to get to the top. The whole "Star Wars" saga does the same thing. *Catcher in the Rye* never really happened, but it reveals more about male adolescent psychology than any adolescent psychology book.

There are a few other (not insurmountable) difficulties in understanding the Gospels as they were intended to be understood. First, they were not acted out or written down originally in English. They were carried out in Aramaic, a dialect of Hebrew, and were written in Greek—in neither of which many readers of these pages can boast much proficiency. Furthermore, they embody customs and ideas that were at times incomprehensible even to the Greek-speaking translators and collectors who received them from the Aramaic-speaking disciples.

But a thornier problem is that no stenographer followed Jesus around, much less a reporter with a trusty camcorder. A fascinating study is to read the Synoptic Gospels (Mark, Matthew, and Luke, whose general outlines are similar yet all different from John's) in parallel[2] in order to see the different personalities and viewpoints of the three writers and why they made the editorial decisions they did: making a judgment to transfer one complete event to a different chronological time, inserting words the others do not have and omitting some they do have, inserting stories the others seem ignorant of. A good biblical commentary can resolve most seeming disharmonies (except for literalists).

An even more difficult problem is that the Gospels were not written till, at the earliest, 65 C.E., thirty years after the events they describe—and interpret. The closest written exposition of the gospel message was probably Saint Paul's First Thessalonians in about 52 C.E., almost twenty years after Jesus' death and resurrection. The basic story remained a matter of mostly oral transmission because the early community wrongly believed the end of the world was just round the corner (in which case writing it down would serve no purpose). Soon the original eyewitnesses began to die out.

Therefore, the first aspect of the problem is that the final editors of what we know as the Gospels were most likely not eyewitnesses. How reliable is their testimony? The second aspect is that they were written by men who "knew how the story ended" and whose lives had been profoundly reversed by it: the resurrection and the knowledge that Jesus is Lord, that is, Yahweh. How much did the later writers understand about the events that the disciples did not realize as they were going through them? How much did the writers read back into their description of the events theological elements that the eyewitnesses could not have been aware of? Does their "reading back into" (commentary on events rather than straightforward reportage) render the Gospels as we have them untrustworthy? A third aspect of the lateness problem is that, according to most scripture scholars, at times the gospel writers show Jesus dealing with problems we know from other sources were not real problems in the Palestine of his day but did become problems for the later community once it moved out into the wider European world. On what authority did that later community insert those episodes showing how Jesus would have handled new problems he was unaware of?

NOT EYEWITNESSES

The first aspect—the final editors' distance from the actual events—is easily dealt with, provided the reader allows an analogy to modern-day experience. Several years ago superiors asked me to write about five Jesuits who had been martyred in 1978–79, one in El Salvador, one in Brazil, and three in what was then Rhodesia. I had never heard of them before, and the superiors who had made the request were not about to send me winging off to those places to do research. So I ransacked libraries to find out about those countries; I sent letters to provincials asking for names of Jesuits I could write to for information; I went through a whole file drawer of clippings in the national Jesuit office (in Spanish and Portuguese). When I finished, I had a big carton of notes, clippings, recorded tapes from eyewitnesses to the murders, and pictures. Then I sat down to write as honestly as I could these five strangers' lives.[3] Finally, I sent manuscripts to my correspondents, made suggested changes, and brought out a book that recounted, as near as possible, what had occurred in those tragedies—without being an eyewitness myself. If I were able to go back and rewrite it today, it would be a far better book, but that was the best I could do at the time. And ten years from now, someone else could do an even better job.

The same thing most likely happened with the gospel writers. Mark (who was the first) was probably Peter's interpreter when preaching to Greek-speaking audiences outside Palestine. A great source of stories there. But Christian Jews were arriving in Rome all the time: more stories, more sayings of Jesus that Peter had forgotten or not been present for (like the crucifixion), perhaps even a short description of the final days already written by an earlier writer. When he finished, Mark had done the best he could at the time.

Later, Matthew comes along with information missing from his copy of Mark; so he writes a new edition of Mark, for a rather different audience, probably Jewish because of Matthew's emphases. Then Luke arrives, with a copy of Mark but not a copy of Matthew, and some sources common to him and Matthew but not to Mark (a source called Q, *Quelle*, "source"), and he writes still a third version of the same story, for a more literate and highly placed Gentile audience, which one can discern from Luke's more elegant Greek style, his explanations of unknown Jewish customs, and his unique concern for kindness (only Luke has the story of the prodigal son, the good Samaritan, and Jesus forgiving the one thief on Calvary).

INTRUDING LATER UNDERSTANDINGS

As to the second aspect of the lateness problem, it is unlikely that the disciples knew Jesus was the Son of God until after the resurrection. Thus, for instance, Peter probably did not say, "You are the messiah, the Son of the Living God" (Mt 16:16) when Jesus asked who the disciples believed he was. That statement reflected the *later* community's understanding rather than what the disciples knew at the time it happened. They were rigidly monotheistic Jews; how could a man be God? In fact, it took the later church over three hundred years to wrestle with just *how* that could be true, and some are still at it.

Consider another analogy to this "reading back into." Renaissance painters never tired of picturing gospel events, and yet, their pictures are false—when taken in a literal sense. Jesus was not white, European, or delicate. Neither he nor his disciples went around swathed in brocade, with gold plates attached to the back of their heads. Our Lady did not receive the angel Gabriel in the sitting room of an Italian villa. But the paintings embodied not what occurred but what the artists had come to understand about the people and events they portrayed. The symbols they used tried to capture the invisible inner reality of Jesus and his work, not what they literally looked like in actual first-century Palestine.

INTRUDING LATER QUESTIONS

The third aspect—the Gospels showing Jesus solving problems of a later time—is cited by some unbelievers to undermine the validity of the Gospels, when it is not really that serious a difficulty. The church has been doing precisely that for the last two thousand years: interpreting new problems the first-century Jesus knew nothing about or spoke nothing about, such as the longbow, telescope, blood transfusions, atomic war, genetic engineering, wholesale abortion. The church says, "To our best mind, this is what Jesus would have said about this question." These pronouncements are not part of the canon of scripture; they are what is called tradition, part of the living teaching of the church, which is still the physical embodiment of Christ, the Mystical Body, animated by the same Spirit. If we accept that the church can speak in the name of Jesus in the twentieth century, why not in the first century?

"ALL THOSE MADE-UP STORIES"

Therefore, in a close reading of the scriptures, we have to look for three distinct levels of the developing message: first, the original, actually historical events, like the crucifixion; then the obviously fabricated stories meant to convey a theological (but not historical) truth, like the parables that Jesus obviously made up to teach a truth through story, as any good teacher or preacher does; and finally, the events that seem to the literalist to be true but that were, in fact, stories the later community made up (just as Jesus had) to portray realities the later writers knew about the real meaning of Jesus (such as his divinity) but that the persons actually witnessing the events were unaware of, like the arrival of the Magi, Jesus and Peter walking on the water, and the transfiguration.

Separating the three quite different manners of truth-telling in the same group of books is not as difficult as it seems, but it does take more effort than many are prepared to invest (as the quotation from Raymond Brown at the head of the chapter points out). There are any number of reliable biblical commentaries, and the theology department at any local Catholic college or seminary would be happy to recommend one. However, of all three levels of understanding, probably the most problematic segments are those that probably never took place in Jesus' lifetime but were inserted by the early church writers. What justified their taking such liberties?

The three episodes just mentioned (the Magi, walking on water, and the transfiguration), among others, are unlikely to have occurred historically, yet each expresses a profound truth, once one accepts the resurrection and the true nature of Jesus— which all the New Testament writers clearly did, even to the point of dying for their belief.

The Magi appear in only one Gospel: Matthew's version (2:1– 12). We get our ideas of them more from Christmas card art, chic shop windows, and *Amahl and the Night Visitors* than from the Bible. There is no mention in Matthew of their being kings, only that they were astrologers; no indication there were three, except for the three gifts, which ten men could have chipped in for; no statement that one was white, one black, one Asian, or that their names were Gaspar, Melchior, and Balthasar. Yet even those later, legendary additions to Matthew's basic story are true, not in the literal sense but in the symbolic sense: Jesus came not just for the poor, illiterate, Jewish shepherds but also for rich, learned Gentiles of all races.

The point of the story about walking on the water is not that Jesus walked on the water but that *Peter* did. Any literalist attempt to argue for sandbars or massive lily pads or the sudden upthrust of a whale in a lake misses that whole point, which is if we forget our own shortcomings and keep our eyes solely on Jesus, who sustains us, we can do what we thought was impossible. Perhaps Peter did not literally walk on water, but the coward who denied Jesus three times early Good Friday morning went on to be crucified upside down for refusing to do so again. That is a real miracle.

It is difficult to believe that the three apostles gifted with the searing vision of a literal transfiguration—Jesus clothed in blinding light, Moses and Elijah materializing from the beyond, the voice of Almighty God thundering—could go back to being the same thick-headed dullards bickering over who would have the first place in this new kingdom. The description of the transfiguration was, after all, parallel with Jesus' own realization at his baptism, which changed his entire life. But what the story says is still theologically true. Even though they did not realize it at the time, there was an incandescent energy within Jesus that our minds still cannot fully comprehend. Again, the gospel writers were like renaissance painters: this is what was really going on, even if the eyewitnesses were unaware that it was.

All of this is in service of a single insight: if you are going to read the scriptures on your own—and every Christian should—it's wise to have some help, either a course in delving through the strata of the books or a reliable biblical commentary.

The primary task of the scriptural authors was to be intelligible to their own times. To read the Bible as the authors intended requires that our biblical education be proportionate to our other education. No one would dump *King Lear* on students without a welter of notes, yet we blithely dump Luke on them and expect them to fathom it. Just because people know how to read does not guarantee they can read either Shakespeare or scripture with anything more than the vaguest comprehension.

Like forging one's own soul, like constructing a personal philosophy of life, reading scripture takes effort. But it's worth it.

5

THE CHRISTIAN MYTH

If Christ has not been raised, your faith is futile.
—1 Corinthians 15:17

If you are going to label yourself, even vaguely, Christian, it's worth some time discovering what that claim really means. Every myth (meaning system) tries to answer three questions about the human condition. (1) What's wrong with human life? Why isn't life "as it should be"? And, incidentally, why are we the only species that's saddled with such questions? (2) Given the acknowledged limitations imposed by the laws of physics and death, how *should* things be? and (3) What can we do to make our lives happier? How can we make the world and ourselves better, less uncertain? If all of us have been victims of years and years of helpless indoctrination from Christian educators, we should have answers to those questions at our fingertips. Instantly. Shouldn't we?

WHAT CHRISTIANITY IS NOT

In the forty years I've been teaching theology, I've often asked college and high school students what being Christian means to them. A sort of test of their brainwashing. In the overwhelming majority of cases, these answers come back: not hurting anybody, being nice, being generous, being a good moral person, keeping the Ten Commandments.

Despite the consistency over the years, I continue to be surprised at the wretched quality of their brainwashing. I already knew the indoctrination was pretty ineffective in regard to their behavior; otherwise, why aren't they all dutifully lined up for communion at Mass every morning? What surprised me most was their total ignorance—not entirely their own fault—of the very propaganda with which they were supposed to have been bamboozled.

In the first place, Christianity isn't about not hurting anybody. It never says in the Christian sacred writings that any action is okay as long as no one is (visibly) harmed. Nor do Christians have any monopoly on being nice or generous. Jews want to be nice and generous; so do ethical atheists. Only witches in folktales really want to be hated. Christianity is not about being "un-bad."

Nor does Christianity have anything to do with morality, except insofar as it presumes one is moral, that is, as good a human being as one can be, which even honorable atheists want. Religion is about our "vertical" relationship with God—and with the influence of that connection on our dealings with our fellow human beings. Morality is about our "horizontal" dealings with our fellow human beings and our environment, whether there is a God or not. We have to be moral merely to be genuinely human. Christianity has no monopoly on morality either.

Various philosophies and religions may differ radically on quite specific moral questions—the number of wives a man may have, eating meat or worshiping on a particular day, drinking, dancing, women priests—but other than bizarre cultists all philosophers and religious figures have agreed, consistently throughout human history, about the basics of "man's inhumanity to man" (to use Robert Burns's phrase) and the rules for proper human behavior that should be evident to anyone with an honest mind. And no matter where or when on the face of the earth, all cultures' laws do, in fact, boil down to the instructions laid out in the Ten Commandments.[1]

Many who leave organized religion complain that a major reason was "all those rules." True enough, well-intentioned religious

teachers of all faiths tragically overburden inquirers with too
many fine-tunings of the basic, natural, human law. But for the
most part all those rules are trying to tell people what they should
do just to be decent; the rules are explicated for people too limited or too stubborn or too self-centered or too dumb to figure
them out for themselves.

Can you imagine any creed that professed to make people
happy with themselves and with their Creator that preached the
opposite of the Ten Commandments and the Tao and the Vedas?
"Forget God, and take care of you and yours. To thine own self
exclusively be true! Thou shalt ignore thy parents, exploit, search
for orgasm wherever and whenever you can find it, crush the
opposition, foreswear inconvenient promises, and covet—covet!"
(Tragically, one could imagine those rules reverently spelled out
on the walls of a Madison Avenue or network board room.)

All but two of the Hebrew commandments ("Keep holy the
sabbath"; and "Honor your father and your mother") are negative: thou shalt not. The first three tell the believer what he or she
ought *not* to do in regard to God: no false gods; no contempt for
the Lord's name; worship, not work on the sabbath. The other
seven tell what he or she ought *not* to do to the neighbor: no
mistreatment of parents, no killing, no adultery, no stealing, no
lying or perjury, no craving for the neighbor's spouse or goods.
But observing the Ten Commandments doesn't make people good
Christians—or even good Jews. They make them good human
beings, just as observing the Tao of Lao-Tzu or the Buddhist
Vedas makes people good, moral human beings.

Whoever lives up to those principles is a very good person but
is still not explicitly Christian. (See the parable of the rich young
man, Mt 19.) The difficulty with a *negative* law is that there is
always the temptation to find loopholes. One of the most flagrant
attempts along that line I ever encountered was a boy who was
going to a brothel and told me, "The commandment says, 'Thou
shalt not commit adultery,' but neither of is married." He could
have added "or very adult."

On the contrary, the Christian commandments are only two,
and each is positive and asks for action, not restraint: "You must

love the Lord your God with all your heart, with all your soul, and with all your mind"; and "You must love your neighbor as yourself." No loopholes there.

The first of those Christian commandments says that a Christian believes God is more important than *any* creature: money, home, job, sex—anything. If it ever comes to choosing between the will of God and any creature, the will of God prevails, no matter how painful. Parents know what that means better than most: if it comes to doing the truth (God's will) for their child or keeping their child's affection at the moment, they must choose the Truth.

The second Christian commandment does not say you love the neighbor *more* than yourself, but as much as yourself—with the same attentiveness you give yourself when you look in the mirror. And in the parable of the good Samaritan, Jesus declared clearly that by "neighbor" he meant anyone in need by the side of your road, no matter how deeply you are biased against that person. Or, for that matter, how deeply the victim is biased against you.

So, if you consider yourself even "more or less" Christian—because you don't want to hurt anybody, because you want to be nice and generous, or because you want to be moral or to keep the Ten Commandments, you may be a very nice person, but you are not yet Christian.

WHAT BEING CHRISTIAN IS

First, precision: I am not yet speaking of Catholicism. I am speaking of the core message of Christianity, which later was elaborated into somewhat different interpretations of that basic message: Catholicism, Eastern Orthodoxy, Anglicanism (Episcopalianism), and the various forms of Protestantism (Baptist, Presbyterian, Congregationalist, and so forth). I am examining, rather, the basic message of Christ about which *all* those differing interpretations would *agree*. Time for their differences in the next chapter. At this point, they'd just get in the way.

I am limiting myself here pretty much to the Apostles' Creed, without even getting tangled up in its more refined but nonetheless secondary elements, such as a clear understanding of "conceived by the Holy Spirit," the Trinity, the virgin birth, or "descended into hell."

> I believe in God,
> the Father Almighty,
> Creator of heaven and earth,
> and in Jesus Christ,
> his only Son, our Lord,
> who was conceived by the Holy Spirit,
> born of the Virgin Mary,
> suffered under Pontius Pilate,
> was crucified, died, and was buried.
> He descended into hell.
> On the third day, he rose again from the dead.
> He ascended into heaven,
> and is seated at the right hand of the Father,
> from thence he shall come to judge the living
> and the dead.
> I believe in the Holy Spirit,
> the holy catholic church,
> the communion of saints,
> the forgiveness of sins,
> the resurrection of the body
> and life everlasting.
> Amen.

There, I think, is the distillation of the Christian myth, the Christian life view. These elements differentiate Christianity from atheist humanism and the other great world religions, including even Judaism, from which it arose. A Christian believes (1) Jesus is the embodiment of God. Who knows how, but somehow God himself became fully human in order to show us how to do it. (2) Jesus/God died in order to rise again to share with us not only the triumph over death but also to share with us the divine aliveness even now: grace. (3) Although our material world and lives are unspeakably precious, they are neither as valuable nor as permanent as our souls—the spark of the Divine in us. Thus, when the spiritual conflicts with the material, we want the spiritual to win—at least we *want* it to. (4) We openly manifest our Christian belief in a weekly meal, at which Christ is truly present, and in a serving-healing community. Jesus has no physical hands or heart now except our hands and our hearts. We are Christ on earth.

Those are, I believe, the absolute essentials of Christianity: the incarnation; the resurrection; the primacy of the spiritual in us; and the worshiping, serving community. I beg correction, but I think every other Christian doctrine is—in varying degrees—negotiable.

If you don't accept those fundamentals, you could be a superlative human being, morally exalted—perhaps even a saint like Gandhi—but you aren't Christian.

THE FIRST QUESTION: WHAT'S WRONG?

To the first great philosophical question—Why do human beings hurt one another and themselves?—Christianity has the same answers as Judaism and Islam. Filtering through the symbols of the Genesis myth to its literal core, human beings are somehow, in their very natures, "bent." Even when we have everything in the world given to us, we are still able to act *against* our own objective best interests. We are—at least for the moment—the pinnacle of evolution of life on earth. We were meant to grow and reach, to learn and love. And yet that very hunger for more becomes perverted. We aren't content to *be* more and more; we want to *have* more and more; we want to be independent of God so we can "do it on our own."

The will of God is, quite obviously, that things grow. One need only look at the billions of years of evolution to see that. God's in no hurry. The stages of each individual's growth from cell to zygote to embryo, from baby to child to adolescent to mature adult are evidence of that as well. But, in order to grow, an entity by definition has to be imperfect. Just as our bodies must grow step by step, so must our minds, our understanding. But we are impatient; not "thy will be done," but my will be done. In the Genesis myth, man and woman wanted it all at once and with total certitude, which is what the fruit of the Tree of Knowledge symbolizes: perfect, certain, in charge. "Eat this, and you will become like God" (Gn 3:5). In the Christian scriptures there are few phrases Jesus uses more often than, "Oh, you of little faith." His disciples—just like ourselves—were constantly hankering for the all-at-once-and-total, for certitude, for miracles, for probing the nail holes.

That, I believe, is the original—and continuing—sin: we are not willing to submit to God and trust God.

We begrudge God holding center stage where, by his very nature, he belongs. We want to make up the rules of the game ourselves. We want to leave our father's house and go out on our own. We want to escape the inescapable fact of our creaturehood. It is, very truly, a violation of the three first commandments of the Hebrew Law and the first commandment of the New Law. We want to displace God.

Before humankind, there was no sin. (Let's not clutter the table with angels.) In order for there to be sin, there had to be the intelligence to see alternatives and the freedom to choose among them. Unlike any other creature—stones, vegetables, beasts—God gave us intelligence and freedom. Only humans are not slaves to their environment, or their DNA, or their instinctual natures. If the environment turns hostile, humans needn't merely endure or die; we have the intelligence to shield ourselves in animal hides, to build shelters, to make fire. If our DNA didn't allow us flight, we have the wits to make wings. If we crave another's den or mate or food, we need not—like an animal—immediately and helplessly yield to those cravings; we have the intelligence to see higher alternatives and the freedom to choose them over lower ones.

But—again by the very nature of growth—that intelligence is always imperfect. We do not know any object or person totally—

not even our most beloved, not even ourselves. There is always more to learn—even about atoms and DNA and the limits of human life. We can never have utter certitude; the best we can hope for is a high degree of probability before acting. There is always the risk of making a mistake, often a mistake that causes serious harm to others or to oneself.

What's more, we are also still fused with the animal nature from which we evolved. Our bodies and our animal selfishness are often in contention with what our intelligence tells us are better, more humane choices.

The pivotal and paradoxical gift is freedom. We are not, as some religions assert, the mere puppets of God. Our ability to flout even what is clearly the will of God evidences that. Every other creature that preceded humans has always and will always perfectly fulfill God's will, written right in the fibers of its nature, a command the creature has no choice but to obey. Only human nature is an invitation, not a command. We are free *not* to act humanly.

Sin is not evil because it hurts God. If God is perfect, he *can't* be hurt. Sin is evil because it insults the Giver of Life; it doesn't lessen God in any way, but it lessens our relationship with God— or destroys that relationship completely, at least from *our* side, even though God goes on loving us. Sin is also evil because it hurts us—shrivels our ability to grow as knowing and loving, the two powers that differentiate ours from every other species and that reveal our specific purpose in God's plan. Knowing and loving are the two powers we already share with God.

Why do human beings hurt one another and themselves? Because, despite the fact we know that we see only unclearly, we nonetheless are free to act rashly.

But why did God make us that way? Quite obviously, he thought freedom was worth the risk, even the risk that humankind might freely destroy itself and this planet. And the reason was that, without freedom, love—the greatest gift humanity has—would be impossible. Just as humans do, animals know the lower levels of love; they know lust, yearning, loyalty, affection, companionship, loss. But they are incapable of precisely the love that Jesus offered on the cross—*the* symbol embodying all Christianity means. He gave up his life, for the good even of people who hated him, who held him in contempt, who couldn't have cared less whether he'd even lived, much less died.

There is a great deal of pain built into that interdependence of love and freedom. For one thing, it means I can't make anyone love me more than he or she is able; not even God can do that. It means that the deeper and more rewarding love grows, the greater power I give the beloved to hurt or even destroy me. It means that I know that some day, inevitably, the beloved will die and be taken from me. And yet it still seems—to God and to anyone who wants to do God's will—that love is worth all those risks and losses. For any game to be exhilarating, there must be the chance one might lose. Without freedom and death—and the possibility of sin—human love would have no meaning.

THE SECOND QUESTION:
HOW SHOULD THINGS BE?

The sublimest irony in the Hebrew-Christian scriptures is that what Adam and Eve wanted to do for themselves, independently of God, by "eating the fruit," was precisely what God had intended to give them all along. At the last supper Jesus took bread and said: "This is my body. Eat this and you will become like God."

The Christian's answer to the second great philosophical question—How should things be? What does human fulfillment mean?—has in large part been answered in answering the first question. The first and indispensable step toward human fulfillment is the acceptance of the fact that we are not God but his creations. When Jesus told us to be "perfect as your heavenly Father is perfect" (Mt 5:48), he did not mean us to be flawless. He couldn't have meant that. If he had, he would have been telling us to try what Adam and Eve had tried and been punished for. By *perfect* he meant what any God-fearing Jew would have meant: not flawless (which would have been blasphemous) but *whole*, all together, knowing who we are in the cosmic scheme of things, our role in God's continuing creation, and doing our best to fulfill that role.

We are not God, but neither are we God's puppets or slaves. Jesus was not the Father, either, but he was the Son—and through him we are God's sons and daughters. Not God, but peers of the realm! Like attendant lords and ladies, our ennobling calling is to serve the king—not accepting slavery but gratefully offering the God who gave us existence free servitude. When Jesus spoke of the kingdom, the apostles—with infuriating consistency—kept taking him literally and were looking for him to establish a worldly kingdom in which they would sit on thrones in rich robes and pass judgment. They were as materialistic as we are, just less practiced at it. On the contrary, Jesus' kingdom was an invasion of this world by heaven—the fifth dimension of existence that will survive our bodies—and our task is to extend the breadth and depth of that kingdom.

The New Testament is the sacred writing that embodies our life view. Unfortunately, too few born-Catholics have ever sat down and read it. They've heard bits and pieces of it here and there in sermons and religion classes but never looked at it whole. Still, just as a single cell from each of two human bodies can merge and create a full human being, those who have studied the Christian scriptures find that you can "clone" almost any single passage and, from it, unwind the whole gospel again. Let me deal with only a few examples here; the overlapping will show what I mean.

The Prodigal Son

This story is not so much about the wayward boy as about the father's eagerness to forgive him. But the story gives the lie to those "more or less" Christians who believe God will forgive nearly anything they do. In a sense, that's true; the father had already forgiven the boy, probably before he had even left the property. But the *boy* was still wounded; forgiveness could not take effect until the boy headed for home. The boy couldn't accept the forgiveness until he acknowledged that he needed it, and that he needed to make amends to his father—not for his father's sake but for his own sake.

Most often, subconsciously, when I used to read the story, I put myself into the role of the wayward boy. However, if our role in the kingdom of God is to act like our Father, then our function is to forgive, just as he does. "Forgive us our trespasses, as we forgive those who trespass against us." And we must be aware not only that the father in the parable forgave, but *how* he forgave: The father ran to meet him. He threw his arms around him and kissed him *before* the son had gotten out a single word of his memorized confession. There was no probing for every sin; no talk of recompense. The boy was home! And instead of a penance, the father gave the boy a party! Judaism has a great deal to say about justice: if your offender has made amends, you must forgive the debt. Christianity goes further: you have to forgive the debt*or* even *before* he or she is worthy of it. A Christian still has a right to restitution, but not to vengeance.

In *Les Misérables*, when Jean Valjean stole the bishop's silverware, the bishop deserved not only to get his property back but to see a proper compensation for the betrayal of his trust. Instead, when the gendarmes returned Valjean the next morning, the bishop said, "Oh, my friend, you forgot I gave you the silver candlesticks, too!" That is genuine Christianized humanity. It goes seven leagues beyond justice.

Somehow, I had always read the story of the generous father, too, with the attitude with which I read folktales: "and they all lived happily ever after." Knowing families, I'd wager the two brothers would probably have their differences for a while; father and sons would come to odds again. But it was worth working out together. Whatever obstacles and squabbles there would be, it was worth coming home. Come home. Then we can iron out the less important questions.

The Beatitudes
Someone once wrote that the Sermon on the Mount was more subversive than the *Communist Manifesto*. It sends the whole materialist-capitalist myth, so much a part of our personal

philosophies, spinning topsy-turvy. To those most impregnated with those very real this-world values, the beatitudes sound not like paradoxes but insane contradictions: "Happy are the poor." Why? Because they're not blinded by wealth and property into thinking themselves demigods; they don't commit suicide when life seems unfair. "Happy are those who treat others gently. . . . Happy are those who care enough that they have cause to mourn. . . . Happy are those who hunger and thirst for a good relationship with God. . . . Happy are the merciful. . . . Happy are the openhearted. . . . Happy are the peacemakers. . . . Happy are those persecuted for the sake of justice."

And Jesus goes on in the sermon to tell us that who we are within ourselves—our souls, the immaterial divine spark in us—is more important than what we wear, or how tall we are, or how many people we are able to impress. We'd all like to claim that we really believe that, but how do we honestly react to reading what the materialist-capitalist myth says will make us happy—a set of anti-beatitudes: "Happy are those who can afford to sneer; they made it on their own. . . . Happy are the cool and invulnerable; they never give themselves away and are never taken in. . . . Happy are those who have never invested enough of themselves in others that anyone can cause them grief. . . . Happy are those who have it all and need nobody, not even God. . . . Happy are those shrewd enough not to be taken in by a poor-mouth story. . . . Happy the cautious, who look before they leap. . . . Happy are those who can nurse a good grudge; it will be a sustaining power source. . . . Happy are those who never stand up to counted; no one can ever take potshots at them."

Which version do we honestly believe is the key to a good life?

The Last Supper

Many vacationing Christians tell me they still keep the Ten Commandments. But they seem to have forgotten that the third commandment says, "Keep holy the sabbath day." They usually ask: "Why can't I just go for a walk in the woods and worship God that way?" My response is usually, "Great! When was the last time you actually *did* it?"

Just as Jesus evolved the doctrine of Judaism, he also evolved its worship. It was no longer enough to sing psalms, read the scriptures, and reflect on them. There was at the heart of the worship of the New Covenant an *action*:

> "Take this, all of you, and eat it: this is my body, which will be given up for you. . . . Take this, all of you, and drink from it: this is the cup of my blood, the blood of the new and everlasting covenant. It will be shed for you—and for all—so that sins may be forgiven. Do *this* in memory of me."

Can't get much clearer than that. That is, if we do honestly believe Jesus is who he claims to be.

And notice how he sneaked in forgiveness there, too, right at that critical moment.

But the two most frequent objections to common worship are very potent and not unfounded: One is, "I don't get anything out of it." The other is, "It's boring."

From the start, I'd say, with only a touch of exaggeration, that any minister who presides in a routine and dull way ought to be taken out and flogged. But worship is a two-way street. In answer to the first objection, "I don't get anything out of it," I would ask, "What do you put into it?" This is also a partial response to the second objection. When one sits grudgingly, passively, halfheartedly, even the greatest message on earth, delivered by the most engaging celebrant alive, would have a hard time penetrating those barriers. The key seems to be our motivation in being there. The word *eucharist* means "thanksgiving," which is an active not a receptive role. If the only time we think of God is this one time each week, if we have never tried to open our heart to God, if we've not tried to serve others all week long, it's rather smug to sit there and "dare" worship to work.

God opened the door of existence to us, the gift without which there could be no other gifts: all the people we love, mountains, growth, talent, family . . . everything. We are back once again at the questions posed by Genesis: Who is God, and who am I in relationship to God? And how should I react to that truth if I want to continue to think of myself as an honorable person?

Perhaps one of the major reasons weekly worship seems irrelevant is that we've grown so used to being spoiled.

The Last Judgment

Jesus gave the answer to the question of the path to human fulfillment when he told us the *one* crucial question that will be asked in the end to determine whether our lives were worth having been lived. On the one hand, despite our greatest hopes, we will not be asked how much money we made, or how many prizes we won, or how many times we got our names in the paper. On the other hand, despite our greatest fears, we will not be asked how many times we were married, how many times we practiced birth control, how many times we masturbated. Only one question determines whether we fulfilled the promise of our births: "I was hungry. I was thirsty. I was the one they called nerd, fag, slut. What did you do about that?"

Again, the statement is so clear there is little need for comment. Once again: anyone by the side of your road whom you are capable of helping is Christ, the victim; and we are Christ the savior. You see, if you're Christian, it's all Christ.

The Crucifixion

There are many Christians who, wrongly, believe it is somehow blameworthy to doubt, to be confused, to be of a mixed mind on religious questions. Quite the contrary. As we've already seen, imperfection is not only built into human life, it's a requisite—perhaps even the most important—component of human life. We have to be imperfect to grow. Doubt is not only not blameworthy, but it's a most healthy hunger that we go looking for better answers than the ones with which we've contented ourselves so far.

Jesus himself doubted. At the agony in the garden, he pleaded with his Father not to ask him to go through what was ahead. And on the cross he expressed a soul-searing doubt, agonizing that he'd mistaken his call, that his Father had abandoned him.

But then: "Into your hands I commend my spirit" (Lk 23:46). One of the reasons I chose to be Christian is that it is the only religion I know whose vision allows a God who faced despair, as I have—and yet gave the ultimate act of trust. He leaped into the darkness of death, believing the God he knew would catch him.

Why did the Father ask of the Son such an excruciating surrender? The usual answer is: to make up for Adam's fault. But, at least in my own case, people who explained that always did it using economic metaphors: Adam and Eve had incurred an unpardonable debt, and only the ritual sacrifice of the Son of God could atone for it. But that analogy is in direct defiance of the parable of the prodigal son and his father! It pictures God as a relentless banker who casts humanity into debtors' prison and refuses to give up the grudge until the last penny is paid. That explanation flies directly against Jesus' own clear rebuke of such vindictiveness in the parable of the unmerciful servant (Mt 18:21–35). That notion of original sin pictures God as more unforgiving than God allows us to be!

What was the fault of Adam and Eve, of humanity? Trying to become like God, refusing to submit to God and trust him. Here we have the Son of God—whose state, as Saint Paul says,

> was divine,
> yet he did not cling
> to his equality with God
> but emptied himself
> to assume the condition of a slave
> and became as men are,
> and being as all men are,
> he was humbler yet,
> even to accepting death,
> death on a cross. (Phil 2:5–11, *JB*)

Jesus—even though he was God—"emptied himself." He freely became (if you will allow a limping analogy) "amnesiac" about his being God and his divine powers, and he had to learn who he was and what his mission in life was, just as all human beings must learn to do, one step at a time.[2]

Despite even the scriptural references, the writings of the church fathers, and our catechism instructions, can we if only for a moment stop depending on a doctrine of atonement, a ransom (which is paid only to a *hostile* power)? Without denying or abandoning those insights, can we at least for a while ignore them? Can we begin to see the sacrifice of the cross not as an act of reparation to a Creator horribly insulted at the very outset of the human experiment and wrapped in cold indignation, and begin to see it instead as a total act of *love*? Can we see that history-making action of God thoroughly embodying his enchantment with humanity? Doesn't it say, "See, you passersby! Is there any love as deep as this? Is *this* enough to convince you how important you are to me? How much more precious you are than the trivial distractions that so easily seduce you?"

The crucifixion is undeniably repellant. Saint Paul says, "We preach Christ crucified: a stumbling block to Jews and foolishness to Gentiles" (1 Cor 1:23). The symbol that distills all Christianity means is a crucifix, a statue of the corpse of a man executed for blasphemy under the guise of treason. A genuine Christian looks at that figure and says: "Yes. That is the most perfectly fulfilled human being who ever lived, caught at the moment of his greatest triumph. I want to be like him."

If those who educated us in our faith offered us anything more soothing and less challenging than that, it's no wonder so many professed believers aren't yet aware of what Christianity really entails.

Resurrection

There is only one utterly crucial point in the entire New Testament: the resurrection. "If Christ has not been raised, your faith is futile" (1 Cor 15:17). Was it an actual historical event? Was it a cluster of stories the early church made up (as Jesus made up parables) to tell a supra-historical truth inaccessible to anyone who hadn't directly experienced it? Or was it simply a story made up by the first disciples for whatever purpose: self-promotion, money, simple wickedness?

In contrast to the rest of the Gospels about Jesus' public life—especially the separate but quite similar versions of the passion—the resurrection accounts are quite disparate. Mark ends with the women's fear at the empty tomb (16:8); the rest of his version (an appearance to Magdalene, then to two disciples, then to the eleven and a brief mention of the ascension—16:9–20) is almost surely a second-century addition. In Matthew, Jesus appears to the women, but the main appearance is on a hill in Galilee. In Luke, everything seems to happen on Easter Day, though the same author, in Acts, has a sequence over forty days. John recounts appearances both in Jerusalem and Galilee.

Despite the discrepancies, there are a remarkable number of common features. In all versions the first witnesses are hardly easy to convince: Magdalene mistakes him for a gardener (Jn 20:15), Thomas insists on probing Jesus' wounds (Jn 20:25), the two disciples on the road to Emmaus travel some time with the risen Jesus and don't recognize him until he breaks bread with them (Lk 24:30). In all versions Jesus has to admonish them not to be afraid. And why not? Despite our own lifelong claim of accepting the fact of resurrection, we ourselves would be stunned to immobility if someone we love who'd died suddenly materialized at dinner.

The fact of the empty tomb seems never in question, only whether it was a matter of deceit by the disciples. No one even claimed to have witnessed the resurrection itself; if they'd wanted to fake up a real Spielberg event with rocks blasting away, they could have. But they didn't. The first and principal witnesses were women—who were not reliable enough for a court of law. Why not fudge that easily manipulated detail? And do people die for what they know is a hoax? Especially without any tangible hope of reward?

The writers show, without exception, that the apostles themselves refused to believe it at first. And yet, that same group of cowards who had huddled in terror in the upper room on Good Friday were out in the streets—within a couple of months—

fearlessly shouting about their experience with the risen Jesus. A *quantum-leap* change. What's more, Saint Paul, who had been a fierce enemy to early Christians, nonetheless testified that even he had an experience of Christ risen and was converted. And many of them went to ghastly deaths rather than deny that experience. Every one of those deaths was a death-bed confession. I tend to believe in those.

Could they have been deluded, then? After all, on November 18,1978, men, women, and children in Guyana submitted to convulsive suicide at the order of a madman named Reverend Jim Jones. In 1997, Marshall Herff Applewhite convinced others to commit suicide in order to board a space ship behind the Hale-Bopp comet. Convincing people to die for you takes less magic than one might suspect, as Hitler also proved.

But there is a great difference. The Gospels are an open record of what Jesus and his disciples believed: it is calm, life-giving, and self-sacrificial only to give one's *living* for the neighbor. Moreover, the descriptions in Acts of the disciples' frequent escapes from authorities are evidence enough they did not run suicidally to martyrdom.

A crucial piece of evidence is that, unlike the doctrines of Jones and Applewhite, the teachings of Jesus are still persuasive, in the face of all the odds. Despite being strict monotheistic Jews, the writers were driven by their experience of the risen Christ to use God-language about him—even though they had dealt with him in the very recent past as an ordinary man. They referred to this Nazareth carpenter in words Jews had always reserved, with fierce exclusivity, for God himself, the word *Lord* (Hebrew *YHWH*, or, since God's name was unspeakable, *Adonai*; Greek *Kyrios*). In Mark, the first written life (ca. 65 C.E.), the entire structure of the book builds to the climactic moment when the high priest faces Jesus with the critical question: "Are you the Christ [the anointed king of Israel], the Son of the Blessed One [YHWH]?" (Mk 14:61). And Jesus answers with the unspeakable name: "I AM"—an allusion to the self-identification of Yahweh in his reply to Moses, "I am who am" (Ex 3:14). Even earlier, Saint Paul had written in Philippians (ca. 61 C.E.):

> At the name of Jesus every knee should bow,
>   in heaven and on earth and under the
>   earth,
> and every tongue confess that Jesus Christ is
>   Lord. (Phil 2:10–11)

The greatest miracle attesting to Jesus' resurrection is that a small band of dispirited men and women transformed into a people who "turned the world upside down" (Acts 17:6, *KJV*).

This innermost core of the Christian myth is, of course, utterly meaningless and irrelevant to many today who are spellbound in the illusion that death is, itself, nearly an illusion. Who can value resurrection if death has no perceived reality? After a while, despite death's omnipresence in the media—or more likely because of it—we become as impervious to death as we are to the shriek of sirens or the insult of graffiti or the scarcely smothered rage in a subway car. For those who have difficulty finding Christianity valuable or frequent worship a necessity, that self-protectiveness might be part of the reason.

For those whose (expressed, if not genuinely felt) problems with the faith deal with more arcane mysteries like the Trinity or the virgin birth or the living arrangements in heaven and hell, they are doing battle way out on the outskirts of the essentials: the incarnation, the resurrection, the immaterial kingdom, the worshiping and serving community. The Trinity, for instance, makes the incarnation at least remotely comprehensible. To put it bluntly, if the only God was in Mary's womb, was he sustaining the universe from in there? How could such a person suffer doubt, as every human—by nature—must? As for the virgin birth, it seems a small challenge for the One who brought the universe out of nothing to quicken a single ovum without a sperm. And trying to scope out the accommodations in the afterlife is as silly as trying to assure the particulars of our children's futures. If we really trust Jesus, he revealed God as a Father kinder and more provident than any other: "Which of you fathers, if your son asks for a fish, will give him a snake instead?

Or if he asks for an egg, will give him a scorpion?" (Lk 11:11–12).

King Arthur solved the question of precedence by making his table round, with no one sitting "at the head." God is, quite likely, even smarter than King Arthur.

THE THIRD QUESTION:
HOW TO SET THINGS RIGHT?

The Christian answer to the third great philosophical question—What can we do to make things more the way they should be?—is relatively easy, at least to state, though not to do: we pattern our lives, choices, and attitudes on the life, choices, and attitudes of Jesus Christ.

"I am the way." Not the bridge over troubled waters over whom we have merely to walk. Not the gate of heaven we just manage to slip through in order to be "safe." No. I am the way human living is *done*.

Before going further, it might be wise to uproot an obstacle I have often found to faith in—or even giving a fair hearing to—the message of Jesus: the physical image we have of him. Most born-Catholics I know have based their image of Jesus—the sort of picture they'd draw of him—far less on the person described in the Gospels than on religious art and films. Perversely, those pictures—being more easily accessible than sitting down and reading the Gospels themselves—actually get in the way of seeing Jesus as the disciples saw him.

In most religious art—even in some of the best executed—Jesus is pictured as lean to the point of gauntness, pale, and nearly always sad looking, with long, tapering fingers. And almost always with blue eyes. But Jesus was a Jew who spent most of his life in the sun. He was a carpenter for over twenty years. He couldn't possibly have looked like that.

Worse than being lies, those pictures—like all lies—are dismaying. Even the best intentioned of us tend to judge a person's personality and character, at least at first, by his or her looks. Thus, subconsciously, we have a kind of polite hesitation about pursuing this holy-card Jesus very far. He is made to appear aloof; wimpish; scarcely human, much less male. (In *Jesus Christ Superstar* and *The Last Temptation of Christ,* we see a Jesus who is almost unrelievedly whining. The Jesus in *The Passion of the Christ* depends more on the sense of Jesus the viewer brings to the film than what the film itself reveals of him.) If people of shaky faith find Christ only in pictures and not in the Gospels themselves, it's little wonder they find him irrelevant—to say nothing of being a very unpromising hero on whom to base one's whole life.

The cause of such blatantly untrue pictures is that the artists and filmmakers have pictured, not the Jesus who was, but the Jesus they want (reductionism). They have isolated only the (very true) gentle, meek, turning-the-other-cheek, forgiving, Good Shepherd aspects of Jesus: in short, a pushover. The Jesus who only cherishes. Jesus is a model for good, noncombative, biddable children—but hardly for grownups in a dog-eat-dog world. In order to do that, they have to ignore a substantial part of the Gospels: the Jesus who also challenges.

To give credit to those who hanged Christ, they didn't crucify him because he was gentle, meek, and so on. Why execute an irrelevance? They killed him because he was—in their own words to Pilate—a rabble-rouser. He wouldn't shut up. He assaulted the clergy of his religion with such highly uncomplimentary terms as "hypocrites," "whited tombs," "vipers," among others (Mt 23). He refused to show the deference "due to" men of position, wealth, and power. His enemies accused him of being "a glutton and a drunkard" (Mt 11:19) who went to parties in highly disreputable company. When confronted with argumentative traps, he used an ironic humor that offended serious-minded people. With nothing but a whip of small cords and his own outraged indignation, he drove the materialism-mongers out of the Temple.

It's impossible to imagine the wimpish person in hymns and holy pictures doing those things. But it is quite possible to imagine a shrewd man like Judas and a tough-skinned man like Peter following the kind of man I've described. And that is the Jesus you find in the rest of the Gospels.

What, then, do the life, choices, and attitudes of Jesus tell us about what we must do to lessen human suffering, disappointment, and despair?

Jesus was a man of courage. He stood up to be counted. He was confident (*fides*, "faith"). But his confidence did not come solely from his own undeniable wholeness. As he said himself, again and again, his power came not from him but from his Father (see Jn 12:49). None of us is without shortcomings, but God can work miracles even with mud and spit—if we're willing to submit to him and trust him. We will not be effective because we ourselves are so powerful, but because we have been chosen by One who is.

"He emptied himself." The first requirement is to forget oneself, not only one's shortcomings but one's deserts: "What about me?" As Jesus said, we will never find out who we are until we accept ourselves as we are and get those questions out of our way. That's difficult, as is any act of trust, like leaping from the porch and trusting our father will catch us. But it is not a blind leap. Our father has rarely let us down. It's a calculated risk, an educated bet.

Vulnerability is one of the most frightening requirements of believing in God; it leaves us open and receptive to unexpected requests. It asks us to be properly humble about the extent to which we can see the truth and the extent to which we can understand it. Vulnerability is also one of the most frightening requirements of Christianity: not my will, but your will be done. It asks us to act like adults with others but like children before God. Our Lady's Magnificat tells why: "The hungry he has fed, and the rich he has sent, empty, away" (Lk 1:53). God cannot feed us if we feel no hunger. If we satisfy the hunger of our soul with the junk food of busyness, relentless music, mind-numbing games, trophies, pay raises, power, God is helpless.

Jesus was most definitely more than "un-bad," nice, generous, moral. And he went beyond the Ten Commandments: "You have heard . . . 'Do not murder.' . . . But I tell you . . . anyone who says 'You fool!' will be in danger of the fire of hell" (Mt 5:21–22, *NIV*). And he turned those commandments positive, closing all the loopholes so beloved of the fainthearted. Nothing could keep him from loving the Father, not even the threat of death, and he reached out to all the people he met, no matter how stubbornly they tried to avoid him, even Judas, after Judas had already taken money for his betrayal.

Assuredly, in free servitude Jesus gave his Father center stage. He was a man who—to the limit—trusted not only his Father when he felt abandoned by him, but also us, even when we do not love him in return, even when he doesn't "get anything out of it." That is the very definition of the most difficult and most precious love: the love given when one *doesn't* get anything out of it. If we will allow him to give it, his forgiveness is ours. Till then, he will continue to serve, even the undeserving.

Both his message and his own living of it prove that wealth is far less important than our society holds it to be, far less important than our souls—our "who we are," independent of such fragile and temporary defenses.

His very last act was freely to surrender everything he was to his Father. *Jesus Christ Superstar* doesn't show that surrender, nor, in the script for the original production, is the actor who played Jesus allowed a curtain call. He doesn't come back.

If, at least for the moment, we put aside all the holy cards and biblical films, all the homilies and ill-remembered religion classes, and discover the real Jesus in the Gospels themselves, we find a remarkably fascinating, challenging person. If we line up his doctrine side by side with the myth system embodied in those anti-beatitudes, we find that Jesus was, in fact, a subversive.

The great writer G. K. Chesterton, commenting on Christianity, wrote: "The problem with Christianity is not that it's been tried and found wanting. It's that it has been found difficult and left not tried at all."

6

THE IMPERFECT CHURCH

All the boats leak. The only question is,
which boat leaks least?
—WALTER KUHN

Anyone who finds no difficulties in the ways organized religion embodies the Christian myth is enviable—but only the way aborigines are enviable because they aren't frustrated with poor TV reception or delayed airplanes or uncooperative can openers. Previously, we've faced at least some surface obstacles in communal religion and worship ("I don't get anything out of it. It's boring.") But there are other neuralgic points, of varying seriousness, any one of which could prove a major stumbling block and, all together, could seem like the Maginot Line.

Why can't I be a Christian by myself—or at least with just a few neighborhood friends and relatives? I've got almost nothing in common with most of those people on Sunday. They're all wrapped up in themselves and their own families. And almost everybody must realize the greeting of peace before communion is phoney, strictly formal, insincere.

Even if I'm more or less convinced by Jesus and the gospel, why be Catholic? Other Christian denominations aren't so corseted in rules and guilt, guilt, guilt. They're a lot more respectful of people's privacy in sexual matters, and their ministers know their place. Unlike a lot of priests, they're there to serve, not to dominate. And they don't deny ministry to women while at the same time wearing dresses themselves.

And what about all the internal bickering? Liberals and conservatives, abortion, stem cells, birth control, celibacy, women priests, blah blah blah. Instead of one face, Catholics put forward a thousand antagonistic faces to every problem. And on the other end, the Vatican's always landing on theologians and gagging them for what at least the papers seem to show is just common sense. Why spend so much time, nervous energy, and scholarship on picky precision that should interest only theologians? Why lob grenades at people on *our* side when there's so much need and hurt and wickedness out there begging to be healed?

Take the long view, too. In two thousand years the church—or at least a significant number of its loftier members—has managed to cause enough tragedy to make God wash his hands of the whole enterprise, as he did in Noah's time, and start over in a different universe. The Inquisition, the Crusades, the Renaissance popes, Galileo, Bloody Mary, the Index of Forbidden Books. And the beat goes on! The recent molestation charges against priests—and the coverup. Talk about corruption. Christ himself said, "By their fruits you shall know them" (Mt 7:16) and "By this all men will know that you are my disciples, if you love one another" (Jn 13:35). As the high priest said at Jesus' trial, "We need no more witnesses" (Mk 14:63).

To get perfectly concrete: Why should we credit any statement from an authority blind enough to say any sex between married people with children who use artificial means to prevent more children (for whom they simply can't provide properly) is a mortal sin, that is, an offense against God sufficient to wipe out any claim to relationship with him, a violation deserving the same sanctions as a couple who bomb an orphanage or strangle children at birth? Did any of these learned men ever take a hard look at the way Jesus dealt with human weakness, *especially* in the area of sexuality?

It appears I have my work laid out for me.

THE SOLITARY CHRISTIAN

The solitary Christian is a contradiction. Beyond doubt, Jesus not only gathered a group of disciples but he also sent them out to gather others (Mt 24:14; 28:19; Mk 11:17; 13:10; Lk 14:23; 24:47, among others). Being Christian is, from the clear intentions of its founder, both communal and apostolic. Deny that as you will, but you can't then legitimately call yourself Christian. Even cloistered contemplatives are part of a participative, outreaching church. Saint Thérèse of Lisieux, a cloistered nun, is co-patron of foreign missionaries, along with Saint Francis Xavier who ventured all the way round the world from Europe to the Far East.

The two basic human questions—Who am I? How do I fit into all this?—have persisted since the caves. We want to be autonomous but not *too* autonomous. We don't want to face the battle of life all alone, or even with only a few tested friends. We can accomplish much more, and much more easily, with numbers— with a pooling of very disparate talents and resources.

Accepting an involving, serving dimension of Christ's message depends on the individual's willingness to contribute to a communal enterprise—at the cost of conceding total independence. It also depends on the managers' imaginative deployment of each individual's unique contribution. If, just for an example, a parish resolved to buy and refurbish a house for a poverty-level family, it could embody the communal identity of the parishioners admirably: lawyers, bankers, accountants, fund-raisers, architects, carpenters, interior designers, seamstresses. Even little kids could pick up trash.

Many parishes are offering opportunities for a sense of a serving community in marriage and engagement encounters, group sharing for the divorced and bereaved, and visitors to the hospitalized and shut-ins. The possibilities are as open as our shared imaginations.

As for worship, if I take time to ponder (perhaps during a boring Mass), I almost certainly have a great deal in common with all those other people. I can guess they may feel gratitude for the gift of life, their spouses, their children. I can imagine that, like me, they sometimes wonder what it's all about. At the very least, I can assure myself I'm not the only one who still risks believing in Something larger than my own skin and kin. As for the sincerity of others at the greeting of peace, no individual can do more than guess. The only motivation one can honestly judge and change is one's own.

WHY CATHOLIC?

Other Christian traditions surely connect their members to God, which is the root meaning of *religion*. To say their relationship with God is any less authentic or intense or efficacious is insulting and arrogant, making ill-founded judgments reserved only to God.

Many Catholics seem too condescending, too close to sneering at "lesser churches" posturing in the shadow of the One True Church. Still others begin to wonder if they haven't been stranded by their parents in this particular (and snobbish) mode of Christianity that they never personally accepted and now have a hunch may be quite deficient. Then why not give other viewpoints into the same message fair consideration? There are encyclopedias and Internet sites aplenty. Maybe even attend a service or two, meet churchgoers, and talk with them. (Which could be more scrutiny than most have truly given Catholicism.) Almost certainly you will find, like Goldilocks, some are too hard, some too soft, and one or two—though hardly "just right"—seem at least closer to what Jesus was probably projecting in his ideas of a kingdom. You can be certain that the most exalted ideal can't escape being riddled with imperfections if it has been institutionalized by human beings incapable by definition of flawlessness. Ideals are like the North star, guides, not attainable goals.

Orthodox, Protestant, and Anglican traditions are all holy and trace their origins back to the church of the apostles. Only a fanatic or a hair-splitter could deny that. But Orthodox seem (at least to me) too ethnically divided, and—to be honest—their liturgies are more than twice too long for my faith. Nor do I feel at home with what I can understand of the Lutheran doctrine of total human depravity, despite the sacrifice of Jesus. There is, surely, a real truth in that claim. Consider *Lord of the Flies*, which shows the savagery lurking just below the civil veneer of a group of marooned British boys, aching to burst out and reveal their primal corruption. I've taught high school boys too long to deny that truth. Nonetheless, that same experience prepares me to stand staunchly against that insight, too. It is too reductionist. It fails to reflect the goodness, kindness, the reparability much more deeply rooted than the meanness. More, Protestantism isn't *a* church but many churches, separated from one another by what seem (to me) less than focal issues. And as I will discuss in a moment, most of their rituals don't even claim to transform down to the depths of our souls, but only to "remind." Anglicans seem far readier to make allowances, but their very flexibility seems (to me) *too* diverse, *too* adaptable.

At bottom, anyone must admit the historical fact that Catholicism didn't "leave" Orthodoxy in 1054, nor Luther in 1517, nor Henry VIII in 1534. No matter from what angle and beneath what deforming encrustations, it appears the Church of Rome is the original.

There are flaws in the Catholic Church too numerous to list, as there are flaws aplenty in the last 250 years of institutionalizing the dream of the American Constitution, but none of them alone or even all taken together is enough to destroy the whole, to make me pull up my roots and set them down somewhere else. Overall, my own personal reasons for remaining Catholic (despite all its flaws) are these:

- The Roman Church at least seems the original from which the others branched. Whether scrupulous historians can find incontestable proof of legal transmission of power from one pope to the next is hardly important to someone content with a high degree of probability. Reforming the original, though daunting, seems more promising than breaking away and starting over. As we've seen, God did do that in the time of Noah, yet things seem to have settled pretty quickly back to business as usual.

- The pope is, for me, a father who unites all disparate views with a reassuringly single voice and direction. I confess strong disagreement with popes on specific issues, but I have a conviction we're all in the same boat with a single hand on the tiller. If I grumble about the captain occasionally, that's both natural and healthy, because upper management needs opinions challenging its own, and I'm still willing to swab the deck or climb the ratlines with my fellow crew members. I distrust anyone who invokes inflexible certitude. That seems to me an unhealthy and blasphemous stance for any human being. If that makes me a "cafeteria Catholic," so be it.

- A critical issue (for me) is the Real Presence of Christ in the Blessed Sacrament. Apparently both Martin Luther and Henry VIII still clung to that, despite their other differences with the Roman Church and despite rejection by many of their followers over the centuries. I simply *believe* it, based on the same kind of evidence on which I ground my fifty-five years as a Jesuit, on what Cardinal Newman called "informal inference," a convergence of so many *felt* experiences that they defy logical explanation. But how does the Almighty, Everlasting, and Omnipresent Son of God manage to fit himself into a bit of bread and wine? I haven't the slightest idea. But I accept it in the same way I accept that he diminished himself into a baby in a manger.

The great fiction writer Flannery O'Connor speaks for me on transubstantiation:

> I was once, five or six years ago, taken by some friends to have dinner with Mary McCarthy and her husband, Mr. Broadwater. (She just wrote that book, *A Charmed Life*.) She departed the Church at the age of 15 and is a Big Intellectual. . . . Well, toward morning the conversation turned on the Eucharist, which I, being the Catholic, was obviously supposed to defend. Mrs. Broadwater said when she was a child and received the host, she thought of it as the Holy Ghost, He being the most portable person of the Trinity; now she thought of it as a symbol and implied that it was a pretty good one. I then said, in a very shaky voice, Well, if it's a symbol, to hell with it.[1]

- Probably the most honest reason I'm still a Catholic is the same as the reason I'm still Irish, white, male, and American—none of which I originally chose, any more than I originally chose my baptism or my early Catholic schooling. I'm also fairly certain I didn't choose it freely even at my confirmation; I was a child of seven or so whose advice I would hardly credit today. That was yet another "arranged marriage." But I did obliquely ratify the choice my parents made when I applied to the seminary. Only gradually, though, did my religion—my person-to-Person connection to God—reach down its own roots into the depths of my soul. It's become a friendship, and no matter how unforgivably my Friend seems to have betrayed my trust, like Job, I will not give up on him—because I have the gut conviction he will never give up on me. Without that two-way connection, I doubt I'd be able to go on.

INTERNAL CONFLICTS

Not only is difference of opinion inevitable in the church, it is essential. The church as a fortress is appealing only to reductionists who revere the gospel so much they try to keep it from the slightest "contamination"—and, ipso facto, from enrichment, by hitherto undiscovered sources, like Aristotle, Ptolemy, Galileo, Columbus, Chinese rites, Darwin, Freud, de Lubac, Teilhard. However, openness to cross-fertilization doesn't negate the equally powerful need to preserve the essentials from distortion or rejection. If any find those truths impossible to accept—knowing what they know from other sources—let them depart freely without judicial decision or rancor.

Pope Gregory XV (1621–23), attempting to settle internal squabbles about Jesuits accommodating Chinese veneration of ancestors into the Roman Ritual, wrote wisely:

Do not bring any pressure to bear on the peoples to change their manners, customs and uses, unless they are evidently immoral. What could be more absurd than to transplant France, Spain, Italy, or some other European country to China? Do not introduce all that to them, but only the faith, which does not despise or destroy the manners and customs of any people. *(Romanae sedis antistes)*

Unfortunately, he was succeeded by men of narrower vision.

But we would be poorer without those who still cling as we do to the nonnegotiables—the incarnation; the resurrection; the primacy of the spiritual in us; and the worshiping, serving community—but nevertheless challenge everyone else to consider long-unquestioned doctrines from a new angle. Chesterton said the church is not neat and sleek like a Roman pillar but rather like a huge, ugly rock with all manner of knobs and excrescences, teetering precariously on its pedestal. The excesses of the conservative delicately balance the overindulgences of the liberal. Let the quietist seek out a liturgy with no hymns and the enthusiast find one that rocks. Let us rejoice in a church that is home to both the Little Flower and the Wife of Bath.

As we will see more fully in the next chapter, the insights of science and religion are also not mutually exclusive but complementary. As John Paul II wrote so eloquently:

> The unity that we seek . . . is not identity. The church does not propose that science should become religion or religion, science. On the contrary, unity always presupposes the diversity and the integrity of its elements. Each of these members should become not less itself but more itself in a dynamic interchange, for a unity in which one of the elements is reduced to the other is destructive, false in its promises of harmony and ruinous of the integrity of its components. We are asked to become one. We are not asked to become each other.[2]

The lion can lie down with the lamb without becoming a pussycat.

THE *CASTA MERETRIX*

We can never let ourselves forget that the church has always been known, even by fathers of the church like Ambrose and Augustine, as *casta meretrix* (chaste whore). Despite Luther's insistence that the Roman Church is the "Whore of Babylon" from *Revelation*, that fusion of sin and sanctity echoes the persistent biblical theme of Israel's adultery (David and Bathsheba, the Song of Solomon, Hosea, Rahab [Josh 2]), which never lessened Yahweh's infatuation with her. Undoubtedly there was a reason Jesus was so enlightened dealing with unchaste women (Lk 7:36–50; Jn 4:4–40; 8:1–11). He never scorned them, though he consistently heaped contempt on posturing clergy (Mt 3:7; 5:20; 16:6; 19:20; 20:20; 23; Mk 8:15; 10: 35;12:13; Lk 6:7; 11; Jn 9:16; 12:42).

The *casta meretrix* acknowledges the inherent sinfulness of the people while equally acknowledging the sanctity of the church as the immaculate bride of Christ. From the get-go, the church fumbled the ideal. The first pope denied even knowing Christ, three times in one night, to a waitress. James and John were riddled with ambition. Thomas grumbled in doubt. One of Jesus' personally chosen seminarians betrayed him for money. Vatican II referred to the imperfection of the church, too: "The Church, embracing in its bosom sinners, at the same time holy and always in need of being purified, always follows the way of penance and renewal" (*Lumen gentium*, no. 8).

Face it: scandal makes the news. No tabloid will run an article entitled "Soup-Kitchen Priest Finally Gets Loan" or "Missionary Nun Falls into Bed Exhausted Again." College students would far prefer to write papers on the roaring profanities of Pope Alexander VI or the scourge of AIDS in Africa (rooted exclusively in the church's sanctions on birth control) than research the rise of hospitals and universities in the Middle Ages. Fewer than 1 percent of American priests have been accused of molestation; do they negate the 99 percent? Popes speaking out on social justice are not going to make the *Times*, much less the *New York Post*. What about the witness of the countless leprosaria, schools, shelters, and hospices over the last twenty centuries? We are quick to judge the admittedly unchristian Inquisition and Crusades, but does anyone care to praise—much less give thanks for—the uncountable nameless monks who meticulously preserved the wisdom of Greece and Rome for us, squinting by candlelight to copy word after word that many of them couldn't even understand?

I have a visceral conviction that the incurable itch to seek out flaws in the church is rooted at least partly in the well-intentioned efforts of the church's most loyal apologists to establish its claim to certainty and flawlessness, despite evidence available to any child with access to the Internet or an encyclopedia.

THE ISSUE OF BIRTH CONTROL

There are, indeed, pitiable people who deny the church's epic faults. The same kind of defensive minds also, on one hand, deny the historicity of the Holocaust, and or on the other, shuffle away the truth that the same fanatic purge accounted for the deaths of nine million Gentiles as well as six million Jews. We are back to Chapter 1 of this book: the truth is "out there," and it won't go away, no matter how often and how fiercely we deny it. In the past the official church and misguided adherents have been responsible for what in hindsight was monumentally wrong and utterly defiant of the spirit of Jesus—not to mention objective facts. There must be some value in imperfection, because God made us all imperfect, and presumably God knew what he was doing. And if the magisterium has made errors in the past, the probability exists that it can err again. Forthrightly confessing that truth is not to demonstrate weakness or disloyalty but to exert an otherwise well-founded confidence.

Peter, the very first pope, admitted he had been dead wrong about his insistence on circumcision and the Jewish dietary laws for Gentile converts (Acts 11:1–18). Pope Saint Gregory the Great (590–604), a doctor of the church, condemned pleasure in marital intercourse ("Pastoral Care," 3, 27); Innocent IV (1243–54) officially justified torture of heretics and witches in judicial interrogations *(Ad extirpanda)*; Boniface VIII (1294–1303) wrote: "We declare, state and define that it is altogether necessary for salvation for every human creature to be subject to the Roman Pontiff" *(Unam sanctam [DS 875])*; and Pius IX (1846–78) condemned the proposition "that freedom of conscience and of worship is the proper right of each man" *(Syllabus of Errors [DS 1715])*. The church's position on slavery wasn't officially corrected until Vatican II in 1965 *(Lumen gentium,* nos. 27, 29). And on October 21, 1992, the church declared that it had erred in its treatment of Galileo in 1689.[3]

In 1963, Pope John XXIII established a commission of six (including three lay people) to study questions of birth control and population. After John's death that same year, Pope Paul VI added theologians to the commission and over three years progressively expanded it from thirteen, to fifteen, to fifty-eight, and finally seventy-two members from five continents (including sixteen theologians, thirteen physicians, and five women, with an executive committee of nine bishops and seven cardinals).

Although Pope Paul withdrew the birth-control issue from the deliberations of Vatican II, the Ecumenical Council nonetheless wrote in 1965:

> Let [parents] thoughtfully take into account both their own welfare and that of their children, those already born and those which the future may bring. For this accounting they need to reckon with both the material and the spiritual conditions of the times as well as of their state in life. Finally, they should consult the interests of the family group, of temporal society, and of the Church herself. The parents themselves and no one else should ultimately make this judgment in the sight of God. *(Gaudium et spes,* no. 50)

Mrs. Patty Crowley, a mother of four, with her husband, Patrick, reported the commission's conclusions:

The theologians met separately to review the data. Ninety percent of them concluded that birth control was not intrinsically evil and that the document *Casti Conubii* [Pius XI, 1930] could be changed. This recommendation was reviewed by the entire commission and 90 percent were in full agreement. A majority document was presented to the pope reflecting this opinion.[4]

However, on July 25, 1968, Pope Paul issued the encyclical *Humanae vitae.* After thanking the experts on the commission and his fellow bishops around the world for their input, he nonetheless wrote:

> The conclusions at which the commission arrived could not, nevertheless, be considered by us as definitive. . . . The Church, calling men back to the observance of the norms of the natural law, as interpreted by their constant doctrine, teaches that each and every marriage act (quilibet matrimonii usus) *must remain open to the transmission of life.* (nos. 6, 11)

Speaking at a November 1988 meeting of the John Paul II Institute for Studies on Marriage and Family, Pope John Paul II strongly agreed:

> This moral norm does not allow of any exceptions: no personal or social circumstance has ever been, is, or ever will be, able to make such an act rightly ordered.

In 1995, he reiterated his stance:

> Thus the original import of human sexuality is distorted and falsified, and the two meanings, unitive and procreative, inherent in the very nature of the conjugal act, are artificially separated: in this way the marriage union is betrayed and its fruitfulness is subjected to the caprice of the

couple. Procreation then becomes the "enemy" to be avoided in sexual activity. (*Evangelium vitae*, no. 23)

Few could argue about the popes' intention. What became a cause célèbre was definite, vocal, and continual disagreement with its objective validity and the degree to which individual married couples should hold themselves bound by it.

The 1980 Synod on the Family held in Rome fifteen years after *Humanae vitae* reported that

- 76.5% of US Catholic women used artificial birth control;
- 96% used methods forbidden by *Humanae Vitae*;
- only 29% of clergy believed artificial birth control immoral;
- only 13% would refuse absolution to someone who practiced it;
- over 600 US theologians signed dissenting statements.[5]

Fr. Bernard Häring, also a commission member, speaking at Holy Cross Abbey, said that in one commission meeting, Fr. Marcelino Zalba, a Spanish Jesuit,

"cried out, and I understand it was the real anguish of a soul of a good man: 'What then with the millions we have up to now sent to hell, if these things can be changed?' Mrs. Crowley, this nice and gentle American lady responded, 'Father Zalba, are you so sure that God executed all your orders?'"[6]

In 1993 Peter Steinfels conducted a survey for the *New York Times* and found that eight out of ten Catholics disagreed with the statement, "Using artificial means of birth control is wrong"; nine out of ten said that "someone who practices artificial birth control can still be a good Catholic.[7]

In the end, married people are, according to church doctrine, the only ministers of that sacrament (not ordained clergy) and the only ones who have experienced its effects. And, as Anna Quindlen writes, "Anyone who defines marriage largely in terms of what happens in bed has never been married."

Finally, the passage from Vatican II quoted above, declared by a full assembly of the world's bishops and ratified by Pope Paul VI, states unequivocally: "The parents themselves and no one else should ultimately make this judgment in the sight of God."

OTHER NEURALGIC ISSUES

In *Spe salvi* Pope Benedict XVI wrote:

So now we must ask explicitly: Is the Christian faith also for us today a life-changing and life-sustaining hope? Is it "performative" for us—is it a message which shapes our life in a new way, or is it just "information" which, in the meantime, we have set aside and which now seems to us to have been superseded by more recent information? (no. 10)

To all intents, for many practicing members the church's official policy on artificial birth control has become a non-issue. That is true, however, only in the developed world, where the issue nonetheless still writhes beneath the surface of many other challenges to the church's credibility. And I fear that the official church's perceived attitudes are *the* fundamental cause of its own irrelevance or even repugnance to so many.

That out-of-touch attitude appears concretely in the case of the bishop mentioned in Chapter 1, who dismissed twenty-two members of his diocesan catechetical staff, because, despite all the baptisms and marriages, so few young people attended Mass. That disequilibrium didn't seem to make anyone ask, "Why aren't *we* persuasive?" In the real world, when an ad campaign fails, prudent management rigorously criticizes its pitch. In large part, those in charge of the church seem to blame the disinterested audience, who turn to the church only when they feel she has something worthwhile to offer, like baptisms, weddings, and funerals.

The image of the Vatican II church seemed for a while quite different from what had preceded it for centuries, as different as the Copernican understanding of the sun-centered solar system from the Ptolemaic conviction. The magisterium seemed no longer the immovable center of Catholic reality. That change, in turn, seemed to hold out hope for a change in attitude and style. Yet at present, many look at members of the magisterium like red-coated British colonels still overseeing the Indian Raj, Kiplings bearing "the white man's burden."

There are two quite different ways of dealing with questions of theology (what you know), belief (what you accept), and religion (what you do). One is from the "top down," the other from the "bottom up."

The first process begins from a body of doctrines experts are convinced (from thousands of years' brooding over them) are trustworthy. They instruct inquirers about truths they think are unchallengeable in order to give them confidence in an eternal Creator's self-revelations and, more concretely, in accepting what attitudes and actions will guide the individual to a fulfilled life. Any new questions, unforeseen by past experts (atomic war, cloning, stem-cell research), are submitted to the guiding principles in that mass of accepted truths. This has been pretty much the church's approach for the last thousand years.

The other approach (the one used in this book) begins with the inquirer rather than with foregone conclusions. The absolute first question is: Is this quest even worth the effort? Where are you right now, and how can we help you broaden your horizons? This was unarguably the attitude Jesus manifested in approaching his audiences and the one used by the church in the earlier centuries when it was still finding its own way.

The first approach (which seems still the official church's exclusive method) is defined succinctly as *fidens quarens intellectum*: someone who already believes seeking rational substantiation of that faith. A nearly insurmountable obstacle arises with that approach today. Most people simply don't *have* the simple peasant faith they once had when we were cleanly divided into "the church teaching" and "the church taught," in which the latter had nothing to say and the former had nothing to learn.

That obstacle comes not from any weakness in the objective truth of church doctrines but from the receptivities of the audience, especially among people educated to ask the human question: why? On the one hand—within lifelong Catholics who, because of more pressing needs, have been unable to keep abreast of "all the changes"—many doctrines now seem either essentials lost (a feeling of belonging) or peripherals suddenly focal (impeccable doctrine). On the other hand—for the young whom the church claims to be "forming"—at worst all transcendent questions have been rendered ludicrous by a triumphant hedonism, or at best religion is a hypocrisy to be tolerated as long as parents are footing the bills. ("I spent a fortune getting those kids a Catholic education, and now they don't even go to Mass!")

Further, overtures to rectify the disenfranchisement of Catholic women seem insubstantial and condescending. One woman says, "So, I love my church and my religion. But at present, I love it from a distance. Because when I get close, I become a little girl again. Or an angry middle-aged woman. Or a grieving old woman. And none of them can do anything with her feelings." This despite the fact that, with one possible exception, no male had the courage to witness Jesus' crucifixion—and women were the first to witness his resurrection; despite the fact Saint Paul called them "my fellow workers." Surely, we can't still base judgments on the belief that Eve sinned first.

Many parishes reach out to welcome homosexuals and lesbians, but the official stricture holds firm against intercourse, even between lifelong devoted couples, since such union cannot possibly be open to procreation. However, the church does allow that kind of communion to sterile couples who, similarly, have no culpability in their sexual "predicament."

In fairly recent times the church has been aggressively adaptive in pursuing annulments of marriages that have proven ruinously ill-advised—just as civil courts declare contracts invalid when essential elements are not fulfilled. Moreover, of the six sayings in the Sermon on the Mount (about anger, lust, divorce, oaths, resisting evil, and love of enemies) only the saying on divorce has been codified into binding sanctions of law. The others are ideals and guides. A far more sensitive question arises when people who (for whatever reason) can't qualify for annulment are in what appears to be a new, well-founded, loving relationship and truly want to participate in the sacramental life in the church. Their exclusion goes directly counter to Jesus' treatment of sexual sinners: the "woman known as a sinner" who washed his feet with her tears (Lk 7:38) , the adulterous woman (Jn 8:3), the Samaritan woman at the well (Jn 4:1-26). In fact, at least in the Gospels, Jesus seems far less perturbed by sexual failings than by hypocrisy.

The liturgy is the only point at which the lives of most Catholics converge with the life of the church. Whoever came up with that word, which is so like *lethargy*? Surely nobody who habitually sits in the pews. Surely no poet. It evolved most likely from theologians who are also responsible for phrases like "our spiritual drink" and for all the prayers in the *Sacramentary*, not a one of which can move the human heart–especially of someone of fragile faith. Most Catholics feel like "the bruised reed or the smoldering flax" that Jesus promised not to disdain (Mt 12:20), like the field infested with weeds (Mt 13:24), like the self-deprecating tax collector who felt uncomfortable in the Temple (Lk 18:9-14), like the fumbling Peter who felt unworthy even to be in Jesus' presence (Lk 5:8) and yet whom Jesus felt worthy to be the first pope. The church seems to offer us too much theology and too little religion, too much caution and too little caring.

In "the old days," Latin was able to cover up a priest's indifference or lack of imagination– or even, as in *The Power and the Glory*, his patent sinfulness, but now the whole focus for people of tenuous faith (besides the moment of communion) is the homily. If the homily is boring, the Mass is boring, and if the Mass is boring, being a Catholic is boring. Let those who fret for the church of the future take heed of that iron logic.

At great expense and effort the official church generated and published *The Catechism of the Catholic Church,* and the United States Conference of Catholic Bishops (USCCB) has a plan to regiment all religious textbooks: "Doctrinal Elements of a Curriculum Framework for the Development of Catechetical Materials for Young People of High School Age." Both documents, available on the Internet, are resolutely "top down"—exactly the opposite of the process of conversion. In fact, conversion has no relevance in them and, indeed, appears presumed. Passing on the faith is merely a matter of competent propaganda. Given thorough instructional materials and skillful teachers, anyone of moderate intelligence and good will should find faith and worship *certainly* desirable. The truth, however, is that our intended audience is brainwashed from birth to find everything Christianity means not only incomprehensible but repellently naive. Offering faith is easier amid widespread deprivation and death, not so when instant gratification takes too long.

Finally, and for some most corrosively, the recent devastating exposé of priests accused of defiling children is inescapably a "sin that cries to heaven" (*Catechism,* no. 1867). Many bishops tried to cover it up, protected the offender rather than the devastated victims. Although a John Jay research report commissioned by the USCCB found accusations against "only" about 4 percent of all U.S. priests[8]—numbers no greater than those for abuse in other institutions[9]—that is scant consolation for an institution that claims that the "one Church of Christ . . . subsists in the Catholic Church, governed by the successor of Peter and the Bishops in communion with him" (*Lumen gentium,* no. 8). That claim was reiterated in a 2007 church document that states that "subsists" indicates "the full identity of the Church of Christ with the Catholic Church."[10]

How does such a claim dare assert itself in the face of the narcissism that refuses to admit mistakes, the baseless assumption of strong faith in veterans and newcomers, insensitive fastidiousness about sexual questions, the emotional sterility of so many rituals—when the very word *religion* means an intense personal connection of people with God?

There are also uncountable flaws in the way our government embodies the American ideal, some of them appalling, like Iraq. But I'm not about to pack my bags and move to Tierra del Fuego. If you want any perfect ideal embodied by resolutely imperfect people, go search in some other galaxy. Emigrate, or learn to live with glaring paradoxes. The church is a *casta meretrix*, a virginal whore. And she has been that way since before the disciples rose from the last supper.

There is yet another Christian paradox we must reckon with. If we could distill the good news into only two words, they could be *forgiveness* and *resurrection*. Forgiveness permeates ever page of the Gospels. Jesus' nearly final words were, "Father, forgive them. They don't know what they're doing" (Lk 23:34). And everything Jesus said is nothing more than the pious utterances of a God-deluded carpenter without the assurance that life will rise from death.

As we hope for forgiveness, we must forgive "those in charge"–and one another–for being too focused on worldly norms, just like the very first Christians. Vengeance for our injustices belongs to heaven, not to us. But–and this is crucial–we must also remember that Jesus didn't call us to be docile sheep. We're to climb to the housetops and be heard. Edmund Burke wrote, "All that's needed for the triumph of evil is that good men be silent." And Eldredge Cleaver wrote: "If you're not part of the solution, you're part of the problem." If the church is to rise like a phoenix, like our Founder from the tomb, it must be from the bottom up, not from the top down. Joan of Arc, Ignatius Loyola, Dorothy Day, Cesar Chavez, Lech Walesa, Mother Teresa were all nobodies, until they got fed up enough to stand up.

Example: For several months I helped out with Masses in a nearby parish. The people seemed to like a priest who wasn't glum and gave five-minute homilies that smelled of the thesaurus. But one woman in the choir, a member of Opus Dei and a seminary professor, made a list of all my (to me) trivial departures from the rubrics and gave them to the pastor. When I met with her, she said, "I don't want a Mass that's simply valid. I want a Mass that's completely licit according to *The Roman Ritual*."

Because she told the pastor she'd take the matter directly to the cardinal, I dropped out of the rotation. She was only one person, and a woman at that, but her courageous conviction gave her a power greater than the pastor's.

When God made continued faith painfully difficult for Job, he was wise enough to say (before his friends arrived), "Shall we take the good from God and not trouble?" (Jb 2:10). And when Jesus asked his disciples to accept the Eucharist, "many of his disciples said 'This is a hard teaching. Who can accept it?' And many no longer followed him. But Peter [not the ideal disciple, but the typical fumbler in faith] said, 'Lord, to whom should we go? You have the words of eternal life'" (Jn 6:60, 68).

THE PRIMACY OF CONSCIENCE

Cardinal Newman wrote in a letter to the Duke of Norfolk, "Conscience is the aboriginal Vicar of Christ." An honestly reasoned conscience is the pope in one's soul.

Vatican II decreed:

In the depths of his conscience, man detects a law which he does not impose upon himself, but which holds him to obedience. Always summoning him to love good and avoid evil, the voice of conscience when necessary speaks to his heart: do this, shun that. For man has in his heart a law written by God; to obey it is the very dignity of man; according to it he will be judged. Conscience is the most secret core and sanctuary of a man. There he is alone with God, Whose voice echoes in his depths. (*Gaudium et spes*, no. 16)

Pope John Paul II expressed the same: "He must not be forced to act contrary to his conscience. Nor must he be prevented from acting according to his conscience, especially in religious matters" (*Dignitatis humanae*, no. 2).

The Catechism of the Catholic Church concurs, but adds a cautionary note:

A human being must always obey the certain judgment of his conscience. If he were deliberately to act against it, he would condemn himself. Yet it can happen that moral conscience remains in ignorance and makes erroneous judgments about acts to be performed or already committed. (no. 1790)

This ignorance can often be imputed to personal responsibility. This is the case when a man "takes little trouble to find out what is true and good, or when conscience is by degrees almost blinded through the habit of committing sin." In such cases, the person is culpable for the evil he commits. (no. 1791)

Yet again, we are in danger of forgetting the fairly obvious insights with which this book began. First, an act of faith or an act of conscience is an *opinion*, and an opinion is only as valid as the objective evidence and the honest reasoning that substantiates it. One's reasoned opinion on birth control is a *human* (moral) question, not just a matter of whether coldly objective lab tests of a suspect's DNA demonstrate guilt. Second, the evidence contributing to that opinion is not merely left-brain, strictly logical, hierarchical. To avoid "half-witted" conclusions we must also consult the evidence presented or rather *demanded* by right-brain, intuitive, contextual evidence. As with the case of closing our factory in Homeville, the truth is not isolated from very significant correlative effects. The profound—often devastating—psychological burden of having another child (when the couple is already tormented trying to care for the children it has) may not be legitimately left out of consideration. That is a very significant part of the *moral* decision, just as a husband's incessant abuse of his wife and children cannot be ignored if the wife is charged with murdering him.

To frame the basis for a difference of opinion—even with the papacy—in its boldest terms: God did give human beings intelligence before God found need to give us the magisterium. By far the preponderance of all those rules were written for people incapable of thinking for themselves. As the Book of Job proves incontestably, God is not in any way ruffled by our determination to question even *him*! And Job's acknowledgment of the truth came, not at the conclusion of a tortuous logical process, but from a personal, full-person encounter with it.

Incontestably, all the boats leak. But there are still a great many of us who—after many years and constant probing—are still convinced the Roman Catholic Church leaks least.

7

BUT SCIENCE SAYS ...

*Faith is the great cop-out, the great excuse to
evade the need to think and evaluate evidence. . . .
Faith, belief that isn't based on evidence, is the
principal vice of every religion.*[1]
—RICHARD DAWKINS

A few bestsellers today scorn poor benighted believers, attempting to show that science has struck off the shackles of religion for those brave enough to surrender reassuring dependence on an unnecessary God. If science has yet to write the definitive R.I.P., it's only a matter of time before we can rid ourselves of the Watchmaker eccentric, bungler enough to have 90 percent of his creations disappear before he even got around to humans. From the start, we've been self-deluded in grasping onto a God responsible for creating willful creatures like ourselves, capable not only of the Sistine Ceiling but the atomic bomb. As Nickels says in Archibald MacLeish's verse play on Job,

> "If God is God, he is not good;
> If God is good, he is not God."[2]

If the One in ultimate charge really is freely responsible for *everything*, then it defies reason to call him/her/it benevolent, not if you include among his artifacts children born with harelips and bloated bellies in Africa, doomed to agonize for a while and then die. And if that consoling old Grandfather really does exist, he

115

has let a lot of wickedness slip by him from some other sadistic creator.

By no means are all scientists atheists. Quite the contrary. But it's very tempting to believe the really *smart* ones are—especially when we haven't the time or motivation to gather and sift the evidence for ourselves and draw our own conclusions. Meanwhile, atheist scientists like Richard Dawkins, gifted with an engaging style and not gagged by a domineering church, bubble over with bewildering facts. A senior once sneered at me, "Do you think you're as smart as Carl *Sagan?*" No. But a lot more open-minded.

It is beyond denial that God freely allowed encroachment on his omnipotence when he gave humans freedom to thwart his will. It is also clear to Christians that at the incarnation, God the Son freely "emptied himself" to take on the nature of a servant (Phil 2:7). Perhaps our inadequate understanding of God's power tries to crimp God's liberty to use it. As God says, "As high as the heavens are above the earth, so high are my ways and thoughts above yours" (Is 55:9). Now, thanks to the Hubble Space Telescope, we can no longer even imagine how high that is!

For forty years I've taunted high-school seniors with the "problem" of God. Given their only recently evolved capacity to reason and its concomitant resistance to authority, it would be easier to market acne. The ethos confirmed them long before we did—as relativists (up to the individual), materialists (show me), and pragmatists (this on the test?).

But I always held the ace of trump (I thought): the elegant human eye, a near-perfect mechanism whose exquisite parts are pointless without the others. A transparent lens corrects for color and spherical distortion; an iris diaphragm fine-tunes focus continuously, even for impaired children. The retina's 125 million color-coding cells automatically switch among wavelengths. They take three-dimensional, color pictures as long as you can stay awake, and they never need developing or new film. Then images converge into a brain that turns them into abstract ideas! And often if they're damaged they repair themselves! No way could that just "happen," even with a gazillion lucky chances, in correct sequence! As close to God-certainty as you can get!

Charles Darwin himself found the eye a puzzlement. He wrote in *Origin of the Species*: "To suppose the eye with all its inimitable contrivances for adjusting the focus to different distances, for admitting different amounts of light, and for the correction of spherical and chromatic aberration, could have been formed by natural selection, seems, I freely confess, absurd in the highest degree."

To boot, *Meeting the Living God*, the text I'd written, sold over 100,000 copies.[3] Thus, for forty years I was smug as a bug in a rug.

Foolish. Neither avid creationist, willing to negate the undeniable facts, nor defender of intelligent design, zealous to insert God at every chancy juncture, I was just confidently ignorant.

To my chagrin, I found not only that the eye *could* evolve, bit by infinitesimal bit, but has done so—more than once. Defenders of that capacity were not only apostolic atheists like Richard Dawkins and fair-minded agnostics like Steven Jay Gould, but evangelical Francis Collins, head of the Human Genome Project, and Catholics like Brown University biologist Kenneth R. Miller and George Coyne, S.J., head of the Vatican Observatory. Evolution had more latitude than I'd guessed, even from John Paul II's "Truth Cannot Contradict Truth," a 1996 speech to the Pontifical Academy of Scientists, and, before his elevation, by Benedict XVI in 2004, "In the Beginning," an annotated version of a four-homily series on Genesis delivered in Munich in 1981.

It was like the shock I had felt studying theology—accepting that snakes never talked, or that scientists find the Bohr model of the atom, with its companionably orbiting electrons, false, as far from actuality as fifteenth-century maps. Not useless, but quite inadequate.

A severely dumb part of me wanted to find every copy of my book and rip out pages 195–98. More, I've taught it to at least four thousand students, not to mention teachers, who maybe doled out such false assurance. I was Alec Guinness below his beautiful bridge on the River Kwai.

First, the unpleasant facts.

A "sort-of" eye isn't useless. Limpets have just a few pigmented cells in an eye-spot, but those cells are effective enough to sense predators. One step up, split-shell mollusks' eyes receded into pits, and the marine snail, Nautilus, has focus narrowed by a pinhole lens. Octopuses and most vertebrates have sharp-focus camera eyes just like ours. Using computer mockups (and *presuming* a preexistent photo-sensitive cell), Swedish biologists Dan-Erik Nilsson and Susanne Pelger estimated in 1994 that an animal could go from flat-skin eye to camera-lens eye in less than half a million years.[4] Cells had "motive, means, and opportunity."

TIME AND CHANCE

The core assertions of cumulative selection (which, broadly, satisfy our last two popes) are three. First, some element in the cosmic stew has/finds/receives the ability to self-replicate. Quicker than electricity, there are two. When both copy themselves, four. After a mere thirty generations, more than a billion. After two hundred generations, 10^{60}. The second ingredient is that mistakes will happen, despite the hyper-efficiency of DNA (a single gene mutating is often less than one chance in a million). Third, the copies will not be a homogeneous population mirroring the first cell and, therefore, subject to demands of different environments, elements more qualified for survival will prevail.

Major objections come from what chance and time could effect with no intrusion from an Intelligent Designer. Does Darwin necessarily displace God? For a philosopher, *random* means "haphazard, purposeless," but for a scientist it merely means imperfectly predictable, lacking certainty but still constrained within the laws of physics and chemistry—and the particular environment. *Mutations* in a species over vast savannahs of time *do* arise from purely chance "blips" in cell replication, but the *selection* and continuance of those changes is anything but haphazard. Only changes making the host a better predator (or more elusive prey), a more seductive attraction to mates and provider for young, win the chance to continue in the opportunistic game.

A random occurrence is an unanticipated departure from a prior normative pattern of natural events. By definition, unexpected changes are a break from what has been pretty much predictable behavior. That's why quantum indeterminacy on the subatomic level (which defies Newton's everyday-universe predictability) doesn't cause utter chaos. At horse races, experts study the contenders, controllers, and environment and make quite confident guesses about outcomes. So, too, atomic probers track errant electrons, and theologians grapple with the elusive Creator. The astounding rationality of the physical world coupled with the analytic and imaginative powers of the human mind give rise to both science and theology—making educated guesses about unseen causes of visible effects. Annie Dillard, in *Teaching a Stone to Talk*, writes, "What is the difference between a cathedral and a physics lab? Are they not both saying: Hello?"[5] Newton, Einstein, and Heisenberg are like Isaiah, Paul, and Rahner, exploring the same *terra incognita* with the same approximative tools, assessing all the pertinent factors, and making calculated risks. Despite our inadequate grasp of his nature, God would seem the best oddsmaker in the universe.

The sheer magnitude of time for change shames analogy. If the Big Bang blew the first instant of a calendar year, the earth would not form till September 14. First worms arrived December 16, and December 31, about 10:30 p.m., the first humans probably emerged.[6] A new species arising in 100,000 years is regarded by paleontologists as "sudden" or "instantaneous."

DIMINISHING GOD?

When I was on the *Today* show years ago, Barbara Walters whispered during a commercial, "You're obviously an intelligent man. *How* can you be a *priest*?" Not a few Catholics, I think, not merely the young, feel occasional discomfort confessing belief. Someone educated who publicly worships, abstains on Lenten

Fridays, and actually believes in sin seems rather naive. Most of us were trained as believers like lawyers defending an inflexible position, rather than as explorers for truth. A 2004 survey revealed 45 percent of Americans believe God created human beings more or less in their present shape about ten thousand years ago. When many say, "Well, I just take that on faith," they really mean "Are you calling my parents *fools?*" Even our "adult" faith could, paradoxically, deepen if we accept very high probability instead of relying on a "certitude" often grounded on shifting sands, like my eye argument.

Many believers in creationism and intelligent design balk at yielding much to evolution (or relativity or quantum theory) lest it jettison God after such long service, intruding to remedy his mistakes and lack of foresight, like the nearly *total* failure of *all* his earlier species, but also being dependable for miracles today. Atheistic evolutionists worsen matters by reminding us God gave us an appendix with no function but occasionally rupturing, viruses whose sole aim is to destroy, and a world "red in tooth and claw." Dawkins writes remorselessly: "This is one of the hardest lessons for humans to learn. We cannot admit things might be neither good nor evil. Neither cruel nor kind, but simply callous—indifferent to all suffering, lacking all purpose."[7]

In 2004 Cardinal Ratzinger's Theological Commission wrote in "Communion and Stewardship": "According to the Catholic understanding of divine causality . . . even the outcome of a truly contingent natural process can nonetheless fall within God's providential plan for creation" (no. 69). God didn't have to rig natural history so a particular branch of primates began to stand up and look around, any more than he had to steer us toward Babylon or Rome or Buchenwald. As Kenneth R. Miller writes,

> If we can see God's will in the flow of history and the circumstances of our daily lives, we can certainly see it in the currents of natural history. . . . Given evolution's ability to adapt, to innovate, to test, and to experiment, sooner or later it would have given the Creator exactly what He was looking for.[8]

A constantly meddlesome God leads to the deist Watchmaker of the nineteenth century, consolingly purposeful but inflexibly determinist. Our lives would be nothing more than unrolling pre-written scrolls, constantly edited by Someone Else. On the contrary, could it not be that God is more dedicated to freedom than we are comfortable with? He could well get a kick out of watching even genes learning. God's wizardry is in the power and fecundity of the universe itself.

GOD AS CAUSE

Science still yields plenty of clues to a Designer, even though he might not be as intrusive as we've been led to believe. Except for the creation of humans, Genesis itself suggests God's surrender of secondary causality to his creation: "Let the *earth* produce all kinds of animal life" (Gn 1:24). Every planet circles the sun at precisely the one speed that will keep it from drifting into deep space or crashing into the sun, not because God carefully inserted a governor in each one, but because that's the way God, with unfathomable foreknowledge, set up the *laws*—the constants, the constraints, the nonnegotiables—of physics. The four fundamental forces in the universe are gravity (the attractive pull of every body), electromagnetism (bonding atoms), the strong nuclear force (binding elements within the nucleus), and the weak force (radioactive decay). If any one of these forces was even minutely different, humans would have been unthinkable.

According to Stephen Hawking, "If the rate of expansion one second after the Big Bang had been smaller by even one part in a hundred thousand million million, it would have recollapsed before it reached its present size."[9] Conversely, if gravity were weaker, Big Bang dust would have just continued to expand, never coalescing. If the strong nuclear force were a little weaker, no elements heavier than hydrogen would have formed. If electromagnetism were stronger, electrons would be so tightly bound to atoms that chemical compounds would have been impossible. Any weaker, atoms would disintegrate at room temperature.

Miller writes: "As His great creation burst forth from the singularity of its origin, His laws would have set within it the seeds of galaxies, stars, and planets, the potential for life, the inevitability of change, and the confidence of emerging intelligence."[10] God, then, works not in the intimate, palpable anthropomorphism of Genesis, kneeling in the mud to fashion Adam and turn his rib into Eve, but God is—and always will be—vibrant and at work in every physical law that evolution presumes.

Dawkins finds that idea "transparently feeble and self-defeating . . . for it leaves unexplained the origin of the Designer."[11] But the only alternative is that, instead, *matter* was always there, equally unexplained. Our universe could well have broken off from another—and on and on, ad infinitum. Like God. (Enter Pascal, stage right.)

THE MISSING LINK IN ATHEISM

Materialistic evolution claims nothing can exist beyond the world of matter; naturalistic evolution restricts itself to the material world but eschews further questions. Dawkins and Carl Sagan go way beyond their scientific passports. They are disconcertingly learned, sorcerers of analogy, writers of sinewy prose. But when they depart from "how" into "why," they're way beyond their credentials, like athletes plugging Wheaties. To anyone outside a lab, the difference between humans and our chimp cousins is *not* simply a measurable difference in DNA!

Books on evolution ignite questions. (1) The very term *natural selection* seems a misuse of words, since only an intelligent being can assess options and choose. And atheists always use quotes around terms like "carefully rigged" or "discover" or cells "know"—as one would use the words "as if designed." (2) How do we get laws out of luck, predictable "processes" out of brute chance? (3) If what differentiates our species from other animals is learning and altruism, why do Neanderthals still wildly outnumber the wise?

The word *soul* doesn't appear in Dawkins's *The Blind Watchmaker*—nor, of course, does *honor, justice,* or *meaning.* Although he uses *humans* throughout, it doesn't appear in his index, though *ants, cuckoos,* and *koalas* do. Such unquantifiable realities have no pertinence to a purely molecular biologist, nor does his lab have any physical apparatus able to cope with them. They are, however, of profound importance to human beings—who have no place in his purview other than slightly different molecular compositions from chimpanzees.

Even the best Christian philosophers have been content with the woefully inadequate definition of humans as rational animals, no more than apes with implanted computers, as if that could account for a MASH unit treating North Korean prisoners or Teilhard's obedient silence.

Dawkins flirts with being hoist by his own petard. He writes, almost huffily:

> We humans have purpose on the brain. We find it hard to look at anything without wondering what it is "for," what the motive for it is, or the purpose behind it. When the obsession with purpose becomes pathological it is called paranoia—reading malevolent purpose into what is actually random bad luck. But this is just an exaggerated form of a nearly universal delusion.[12]

Gotcha! The core of humanity, dismissed as merely bothersome, like an appendix.

We are the only creatures we know who are aware we are selves, able to use the future tense, to regret. Other animals know facts— that danger is near, for example—but don't seem to ask *why.* They give their lives for their own but not, like us, for a principle or for people we don't even like. Only we have hungers not rooted in a needful body or coldly rational mind: to be honorable, to find meaning, to survive death. Ignoring those indisputable facts is the rankest reductionism.

Charles Darwin, brilliant herald of this astonishingly fruitful theory, was less simplistic than some of his ardent disciples. The final sentence of *The Origin of Species* reads:

> There is grandeur in this view of life, with its several powers, having been originally breathed by the Creator into a few forms or into one; and that, whilst this planet has gone cycling on according to the fixed law of gravity, from so simple a beginning endless forms most beautiful and most wonderful have been, and are being evolved.

Perhaps we might find more *motivated* belief if we were more at peace with intriguing questions than prefabricated conclusions, if we stopped needing to *prove* anything and delighted in pursuing clues.

8

SUFFERING

Sunt lachrimae rerum
(tears are at the heart of things).
—VIRGIL, AENEID, BK. 1, LN. 462

Other animals suffer, lament, grieve, but as far as we know only we are left with the even more agonizing burden: asking *why*. We try to find a purpose, struggle to put the insupportable into a matrix of truths where it assumes a meaning more than the helpless victimhood of beasts. As we saw briefly in the previous chapter, in a view of human life in which God can find no place, that struggle for purpose is a self-delusion, of no real value other than momentarily distracting us from our inexorable annihilation. Atheists who settle for that coldly noble perseverance-despite-death often look pityingly at believers, as if they have chosen the easier, more cowardly self-deception. Little do they comprehend the agony belief sometimes exacts, when the inequities of life have rocketed us far beyond theories and theodicies into naked wrestling with a God who doesn't play fair and who doles out only unsatisfying clues to his unreadable intentions.

Although the very word *purpose* melts the mental circuits of the most ardent atheists, even they can see a worthy function in many forms of suffering—unpleasant realities in the broadest sense, including even leaving the secure warmth of bed to face the further challenge of finding food. A felt purpose gives the sacrifice meaning that at least partly palliates the loss of something valuable, made less appealing just now by a greater good. Psychiatrist Erik Erikson makes a case that the basic structure of every human life is a series of predictable "disequilbriums" that precipitate us (quite unnervingly) from an accustomed serene state into one which offers us a richer, broader, profounder way of being human.[1] Birth itself, weaning and potty training, playing with other fractious children, learning the tribe's customs, adolescence, the intimacy and partnership of marriage, raising children of one's own, growing old—each is an invitation to greater self-awareness, autonomy, independence. We ignore or suppress those challenges at the cost of our souls. And that evolutionary process hasn't changed at all, except on the surface, for the last thirty thousand years. That's why we have libraries.

What's more, there is a curse so delicious many cultures claim it: May your life be . . . *interesting*. May you have lots of fearsome stories to tell, because they're chock-full of unpleasantness, like dragons, fire pits, and howling ghouls. Dante's *Inferno* is a lot more engaging than his *Paradiso*. Unexpected reversals—just as the predictable stages of human growth—can throw our psyches into turmoil, but they also invite us to enrich our humanity. The Greek playwright Aeschylus wrote in *Agamemnon*:

And even in our sleep, drop by drop, the pain that cannot forget inexorably scalds the soul, and in our own despair, against our will, the awful grace of God inflicts wisdom on us. (bk. 2, lns. 219–23, translation mine)

Show me someone who hasn't suffered, and I'll show you an insufferable bore, and a shallow one at that. At the outset of his play, King Lear is a pompous autocrat too used to being spoiled. When he wants flattery, Goneril and Regan lay it on with trowels. What Lear needs is the truth, and when Cordelia and Kent give it to him, he banishes them. But Lear can't escape what he needs: wind, rain, nakedness, to see himself stripped of the self-delusions of wealth and power, as he finally sees the ragged Edgar: "Unaccommodated man is no more but such a poor, bare, forked animal as thou art" (III, 4). Just like Job.

Whether God is a delusion or not, suffering shows us incontestably that we can have no pretensions to God's position.

Nonetheless, suffering (at least for those with the evolved human capacity to reflect on it) is not only a pathway to richer human perspective but also to a more profound human dignity. Viktor Frankl, a psychiatrist who spent years in the Nazi camps, has enormous insight into the transformational effect one's freely chosen *attitude* can have on unwelcome suffering:

> The way in which a man accepts his fate and all the suffering it entails, the way in which he takes up his cross, gives him ample opportunity—even under the most difficult circumstances—to add a deeper meaning to his life. It may remain brave, dignified, and unselfish. Or in the bitter fight for self-preservation he may forget his human dignity, and become no more than an animal. Here lies the chance for a man either to make use of or to forego the opportunities of attaining the moral values that a difficult situation may afford him. And this decides whether he is worthy of his sufferings or not.[2]

A prayer attributed to Reinhold Niebuhr (and claimed by him, although there is some question about versions of it appearing far earlier), adopted by Twelve-Step programs, captures that transforming attitude:

> God, grant us the grace to accept with serenity
> the things that cannot be changed,
> Courage to change the things which should be
> changed,
> and the wisdom to distinguish the one from
> the other.

Difficult as it is to accept, suffering and loss are *necessary* to humanity. Who could value warm, sunny days who hasn't known dreary, rainy ones? Who could appreciate good health who has never been ill? Who would value the people we love if we felt no acceptance of death? Who could offer grateful worship who takes everything for granted, as if it were deserved?

If what separates us from other animals is our capacity to know and love, and if "human" spans a vast spectrum from sadists to saints, then the activities that will allow us the same natural sense of fulfillment retrievers dumbly enjoy from retrieving are activities of "soul-making": broadening and deepening our powers to understand and empathize. Experience is the best teacher *only* if we subject it to reflection and humble assimilation. Then it can make us more resilient, less easily disconcerted, more confidently self-possessed. The people who seem to have made the best of the mixed bargain all humans share seem obvious, not because they stir our envy but because they quicken our hearts: Joan of Arc, Thomas More, Beethoven, Abraham Lincoln, Albert Schweitzer, Helen Keller, Martin Luther King, Stephen Hawking. They built towering souls from the rubble "Fate" had made of their lives.

Arguably the greatest satire on religion is Voltaire's novella *Candide,* caustically exposing the empty-headed optimism of the German philosopher Gottfried Leibniz in his 1710 work *Essay on the Goodness of God, Human Freedom, and the Origin of Evil.* In that work Leibniz argued that, since God is all good, we must live in what is indisputably "the best of all possible worlds." Voltaire offers in contrast thirty thousand people wiped out in a Lisbon earthquake, at least some of whom were likely innocents, and Bulgarian soldiers who don't merely kill but rape, disembowel, and dismember innocent women and children. In his world travels Candide witnesses flagrant hypocrisy in clerics, politicians, and entrepreneurs; floggings; robberies; unjust executions; disease; betrayals; and crashing boredom. In the end, Candide finds the only answer is to shun questioning altogether and cultivate your own garden.

Such biting satire is all well and good for those gifted with intelligence and the training to reason. But what of those without such advantages, who nonetheless share our common burdens and still have that natural human nostalgia for Eden, for a world where things are "as they should be"? What of those without the ability to parse Plato in order to have a reason to keep going, despite the firestorm? What of the infant born without limbs? The family of a father obliterated in a war fought only to save face for a country's *führer* or *duce* or president? What of an only begotten innocent Son, vilified, degraded, and crucified by brutes?

And what of those of us who helplessly watch and empathize, confounded?

There is no need to prove the existence of evil and suffering. It's one doctrine you can establish indisputably from any daily newspaper. The only question is whether there is anything that can explain why it occurs and what could justify it. Some of the wisest philosophers have said evil doesn't *really* exist, that it is in fact only the absence of good. Again, consoling for the learned gentlemen secure in their windowless studies, but of little value to a young mother holding her dead child and asking, "Why?" For her, suffering is as real and devouring as a black hole.

EXPLANATORY MYTHS

From time immemorial, shamans and priests have tried to give a meaningful background to both *moral* suffering (wars, rapes, drive-by shootings—attributable to human misuse of freedom) and *physical* suffering (hurricanes, drought, cancer, death—beyond any human responsibility and imputable only to God, if indeed there is one). In fact, even moral, human evil is—ultimately—ascribable to God, since he set in motion a world where human freedom could be misused.

These attempts at understanding are put forward in myths—stories or theories that attempt (however inadequately) to capture the causes of suffering and ways to cope with it, perhaps even eventually to eradicate it. They range from crude legends to elegant philosophical systems. But whatever their sophistication or lack of it, each is a fallible, human *attempt*, an *essay* in search of truth. Examining some of the more primitive myths might put the Judeo-Christian myth of Genesis into better perspective and defuse some of its unjustified control over our souls.

The Cosmic Egg

The Dogon peoples of West Africa describe a personal creator who began with a great egg. (The symbol also arose independently in Egypt, among some Taoists in China, and far away from both in Finland.) The elements within the egg were intended to emerge perfectly stable, like the dynamic balance of the Tao, nothing in excess. But the inhabitants of the egg grew restive and escaped too soon, leaving the world near chaos: male/female, aggressive/lazy, riddled with conflicts and contradictions.

Emergence

Many primitive Americans, like the Zuni of New Mexico, believed everything was originally a chaos of embryonic beings moving from a potential state to actuality. The earth itself was a child-bearing woman within whom all these unfinished creatures were crawling over one another like reptiles, but some escaped early and as yet unfinished.

World Parents

In the *Enuma Elish*, the Babylonian creation epic, Tiamat is the Earth Mother and Apsu the Sky Father. The earth waters of Tiamat (the seas) and the sky waters of Apsu (rain) commingled as a single body, a perfect, androgynous union. But their offspring were born of "two bodies," earth and sky, restless. They wanted light, space, and freedom, and their rebellion caused a rupture between Earth Mother and Sky Father. A new child, Marduk, defeated the Earth Mother and forced the division to remain permanent. (The Maori, on the other side of the world, have a nearly identical creation epic.)

Greeks

In the dark chaos at the beginning, the only creature was Nyx, a huge black bird who conceived an egg by the wind, and out of it emerged Eros, the god of love. Half the shell rose up as the sky, whom Eros called Uranos, and the other became Earth, which he named Gaia. Then he made them fall in love and have many children and grandchildren, among them Zeus, who commissioned his

son Prometheus (Foresight) to create humans and his son
Epimetheus (Afterthought) to create animals. Being kindly,
Prometheus gave his creatures the gift of fire, which he stole from
the gods. Zeus was furious and chained Prometheus to a moun-
tain where a vulture savaged his liver every day; each morning it
grew back for more endless torment. Then Zeus devised a punishment for all humankind. He gave Epimetheus a devastating
beauty named Pandora (All-gifted) with a wedding present of a
box she was forbidden ever to open. One day when Epimetheus
was gone she opened the box, and out flew all the horrors which
plague humanity. Epimetheus rushed in and fastened the lid, too
late. But during the night they heard a voice from the box: "Let
me out. I am hope." So the two released her.

Zoroastrianism

Zoroaster (or Zarathustra, ca. 350 B.C.E., at the time of
Alexander) taught that the true and good God, Ahura Mazda,
faces a divine and evil antagonist known as Ahriman—thus "solving" the question of the origin of suffering even before creatures
appeared. Although Ahura Mazda is supreme and his ultimate
victory assured, as long as creation endures Ahriman will continue to fight him and bring suffering into the world. This mytho-
logical dualism passed to the sect of the Manichees—a conflation
of Greek, Buddhist, and Christian beliefs, whose founder, the Per-
sian Mani (210–76 C.E.), held that matter was essentially evil and
therefore could not be in direct contact with God. Each human
is a battleground between spirit (light) and flesh (darkness). Saint
Augustine of Hippo (354–430 C.E.), a powerful figure in ex-
pounding Christianity, was a Manichean until the age of thirty-
three. Despite his subsequent fierce opposition to the sect, some
speculate that Manichean ideas on the nature of good and evil,
the idea of hell, the separation of groups into elect and sinners,
and hostility to the flesh and sexual activity exerted too great an
influence, through Augustine, not only on Lutheranism but also
on Catholicism. At its height, Manichaeism was one of the most
widespread religions in the world, with churches and scriptures
found as far east as China and as far west as the Atlantic.

Buddhism

Like most children here in our Western world, Guatama Siddhartha (ca. 563–483 B.C.E.) had been sheltered from even the slightest upset. (A sage had told his father the boy would become either the greatest ruler or greatest saint in India, and his father wanted to lengthen the odds.) But the boy was, naturally, curious, and he sneaked out into the real world to encounter sickness, starvation, and death. After a journey of many years, he finally settled into mere absorption into the power within reality and became the Buddha (the Awakened One). He taught the First Noble Truth: all life is suffering, dissatisfaction; even moments of joy turn into pain when we can only remember them. The Second Noble Truth: the origin of suffering is craving, thirsting for pleasure—even a desire for continued existence or even for nonexistence. The root of all pain is the"self" or "I," with all its desires, hopes, and fears. Through penance, discipline, and meditation, this self proves itself insubstantial, and thus the Third Noble Truth, the cessation of suffering, occurs when the individual fuses with the Oversoul in Nirvana.

To the exclusively rational mind, that absorption suggests that the purpose of life for a Buddhist is a kind of "soul suicide," the self swallowed up in the All. Rather, in Nirvana, the self swallows up the All!

Motifs

Despite arising at points on earth where communication with one another was impossible, there are several surprising constants in most primitive myths. First, at the beginning everything was supposed to be as ideal as our frustrated expectations project. Why is that so consistently part of the human psyche? Second, there was almost always an antagonism between the benevolent creator and the restless creatures. Why is that disharmony also a universal insight? ("If God is God, he is not good . . . ") Third, the conflict is often embodied in two cosmic personalized forces, a basic struggle between the Forces of Good and the Evil Empire. Fourth, the very earliest gods are jealous of their power and punitive. Gradually, over centuries, as chaos yields more to human control, the gods also soften—to the point of invisibility. In Greece, for instance, the very first images of the gods were chthonic (of earth); their bloodthirstiness reflected the people's harsh struggles with the environment and among themselves to survive. Thus, they attempted to placate the gods with blood sacrifice, sometimes even human, in atonement. Later, when leisure gave more time to reflect, those gods were displaced by the anthropomorphic Olympians, a hugely dysfunctional family, given to meddling in human lives and checking themselves in the mirror. Finally, the entirely bloodless, ethereal gods emerged, and in the end the Uncaused First Cause. All of these apprehensions of divinity capsulized the "divine" experiences of the most intelligent and articulate members of successive societies.

Genesis

No need to repeat the story here, but accommodating our minds to the wider horizons of other peoples' myths shows that the Adam and Eve story we first accepted as credulous children is hardly unique. Other cultures faced the same enigmas and came to the same conclusions—and in some cases before "we" did. No matter the difference in the symbols,[3] the insights are the same: we brought it on ourselves, or at least our forebears did.

But just as there are glaring inadequacies and mind-benders in the other stories, so too in our own, if we take it any more literally than we allow those others to be. Are we who have spent from twelve to sixteen to twenty years expanding our knowledge still presumed to accept that at one time snakes actually did talk? Are we to blame all our woes on a woman just as fictional as Pandora? Must we accept (as I sincerely did until my early thirties) that all the negatives in human lives— including cancer, misborn babies, and death itself—are attributable to a single pair of not overly bright nudists in a park who ate *one* piece of forbidden fruit? If all that is literally true, what do I do with the museum rooms in my mind where all those dinosaur bones hulk forty feet high and dense as rock? Do I have to deny that they died before humans were around to blame? If I accept that God "closed the gates of Eden" on humans way-back-when and retired into a nearly permanent grump till Jesus came, how can I accommodate God's unswerving loyalty to Israel for centuries, even when Israel again and again went a'whoring after the Baals? And must I accept that Jesus was a "scapegoat" slaughtered as "ransom" to wipe out that millennial "debt"? Don't we ordinarily use those terms about a *hostile* power? Like all those other creation myths, that metaphor of God as an insulted moneylender does offer an explanation, but how do I square that with the father of the prodigal son, the father whom Jesus claimed God is? When I baptize a baby, must I suppress everything else I believe true and convince myself that this little bundle carries an immemorial "stain" because of the stupid defiance of an inaccessibly remote pair of relatives? I haven't the slightest doubt that, simply being born of human parents, this infant is *prone* to that same rebelliousness, and I want to assure the parents that—no matter what—their child will be welcomed back from any sin when he or she wants. But I can't herniate my intelligence any longer to say a baby still incapable of bowel control is guilty of any whisper of sin.

It all comes down to clumsy, lazy, half-witted use of easy-to-hand words and metaphors.

To repeat: the only question is whether there is anything that can explain why unmerited suffering occurs and what could justify it.

WHY? THE GOD OF ETERNAL CREATION

Reflecting on the previous chapter on the insights of science, is it possible to stretch our images of God beyond the anthropomorphic Zeus on Olympus or Yahweh on Sinai or the Ancient of Days on his smoking throne (Is 6:1; Ez 43:7; Dn 7:9; Rv)? Science says there can be no reality faster than light. But science delights in playing, "What if?" (What if we play around with this bread mold or these silicon chips?) What if there *were* a Reality faster than light? It would be so intensely active it would be at rest. Like God. So swift, it would be everywhere at once. Like

God. And some scientists now claim that, when they crack open the most basic physical particle, they will find "non-extended energy." Like God. Couple those insights with Exodus when Moses asks God who he is: "I am Who AM," the inexhaustible pool of existence out of which everything that is draws its "is." God is present everywhere, or nothing could exist. Would it be any further from the truth to picture God as "three persons made of light" than as a bearded eminence on a throne? "The Lord appeared to Abraham near the great trees of Mamre while he was sitting at the entrance to his tent in the heat of the day. Abraham looked up and saw three men standing nearby" (Gn 18:1–2).

Is it also possible to find in the thickets of science a somewhat less inadequate answer to the cause of physical and moral suffering, some insight other than in the metaphor of a willful people and a vengeful God—which is so irreconcilable with the unadulterated Christian myth? Our well-intentioned Christian training, which depended so heavily on that easy-to-hand metaphor, capitalized on the natural sense of inadequacy we felt in our childhood (like Dorothy at the outset of *The Wizard of Oz*). That anti-human mindset gave rise, for instance, to the Reformers' doctrine of total depravity, by which Luther said the Fall left humanity still riddled with sin, even *after* Jesus' sacrifice. We are still as repulsive as a dunghill that the merits of Jesus cover like snow, so that God chooses no longer to consider our loathsomeness. In Catholicism, too, it precipitated the nonscriptural idea of purgatory and the concomitant doctrine of temporal punishment due to sin—even, according to the *Catechism of the Catholic Church, after* the wrongdoer has sincerely repented and the all-loving God has presumably forgiven (see 1471–98). Purgatory does make sense, if the purpose is not mindless retributive punishment, like school detention, but instead like a long period with a soul-counselor working through the (still quite painful) process of facing the naked truths about ourselves. Rather, its purpose would be to prepare those who die with souls too self-involved to experience utter joy.

What if we started from the God of love rather than from the God of justice? A God we know from Jesus rather than from stories of a rapacious god who expects appeasement? A God who chose to express his infatuation with growth in creating a world subject (within the strictures of the four basic forces) to inventive chance? Saint Paul said, "The whole creation has been groaning as in the pains of childbirth right up to the present time" (Rom 8:22). Are we too well brain-conditioned to resonate to a God who would create and continue to support—*no matter what*— without wanting to step in and control at every misstep? Can we accept a God who does *not* micro-manage our daily encounters with headaches, testy bosses, contrary children, mammary lumps, downsizing, aneurysms? What if we had a God who actually *trusts* in the way he fashioned his creation and his creatures? A God who cherishes spontaneity, uncertainty, risks, gambles, and freedom more than we claim to?

What if this acceptance of openness (as opposed to comforting determinism) were the ultimate condition for genuine love to exist, a love returned to God without the coercion the Grand Inquisitor hoped to impose when God saw fit not to inflict it? For countless centuries humans took their cues from fellow animals: rapacity, vengeance, domination, greed, territorial hubris. And since rapaciousness seemed the way of things, they invested their gods with that same mindless rapacity. Is it possible that the "inevitable" gift of a cerebral cortex evidences an invitation for freely given human love rather than helpless submission to divine dominance?

Does it make us too nervous even to ponder a God so in love with challenge and free choice that, with an infinite foreknowledge we can't remotely comprehend, he saw the ever-so-slow emergence of intelligence and—understanding its dynamic nature as well as he understood the four nonnegotiable constants of physics—set humans to discover themselves just as non-intrusively as he allowed the planets to settle into their orbits and the earth to bring forth life?

Of course, the appeal of this attempt to explain depends heavily on whether we find freedom a more generous gift than security—the necessary cost of a humanity allowed to make itself, just as the universe did.

And no such rational/imaginative essay can do more than make the search for God less of a fool's quest. To wrestle with *proof*, there is no other true way but the way all friends "prove" themselves—not by going to the circus together but by journeying through hell together.

THE GOD OF JOB

The so-called patience of Job in no way justifies the idea of silent, stolid endurance. The real Job spends thirty-five chapters grouching! And it's not his *physical* losses he's mourning most but his loss of *understanding*. He loved God, and God seems to have betrayed his trust, utterly.

What Job yearns for—like the bereaved at a wake or the patient coming out of the oncologist's office or the deserted spouse—is not rational answers but empathy, not only from friends but from the Friend. Job feels God has deserted him, as Jeremiah and nearly all of us have felt deserted. When the Friend himself faced the end on Calvary, he too cried out, "My God, my God! Why have you abandoned me?" (Mt 27:45).

Well into young adulthood, I had a recurring dream that mirrored an actual event in my childhood and that might embody Job's agony. I'm a little boy standing in the driveway, my face shellacked with tears, screaming without sound: "Mommy! Mommy!" And I'm running through lucite air toward the car backing toward the street, my mother's grim face clenched above the wheel. She backs into the street and looks out the window, not at my face but at my feet. She shifts into first and moves away under the arch of trees. And she's never coming back.

I get the same grip in the guts when I read of the seven foolish bridesmaids and hear God growling at them (at me): "I tell you the truth, I don't want to know you" (Mt 25:12, NCV).

Ultimate, absolute abandonment. Forget Dante, whose hell is at least in a sadistic way diverting. Forget Sartre, whose *No Exit* is far closer to the truth: three people who detest one another shut up in a room together for eternity. Even that doesn't capture the ultimate anguish: solitary exile in a featureless landscape into which Mister Godot will never come.

The philosopher Simone Weil describes what the patience of Job really means:

> Affliction makes God appear absent for a time, more absent than a dead man, more absent than light in the utter darkness of a cell. A kind of horror submerges the whole soul. During this absence there is nothing to love. What is terrible is that if, in this darkness where there is nothing to love, the soul ceases to love, God's absence becomes final. The soul has to go on loving in emptiness, or at least to go on wanting to love, though it may only be with an infinitesimal part of itself. Then, one day, God will come to show himself to this soul and to reveal the beauty of the world to it, as in the case of Job. But if the soul stops loving it falls, even in this life, into something almost equivalent to hell.[4]

Before the arrival of his three hyper-orthodox friends to "comfort" him, Job has already voiced the crucial—if onerous—truth: "Naked I came from my mother's womb, and naked I will depart. The Lord gave and the Lord has taken away; may the name of the Lord be praised" (Jb 1:21). And "Shall we accept good from God, and not trouble?" (Jb 2:10).

But then his friends arrive with their unwavering doctrine, insisting God punishes only those who deserve it. But, Job insists (and insists), that if he'd done something so wicked as to deserve this, surely he would have *remembered* it! But Job makes his own mistake: maintaining his innocence as if God were, indeed, *denying* it, challenging God to meet him in any court to try the case. He allows his comforters to skew the search into justice rather than friendship. In all my years of formal study, I, at least, can't remember a single teacher who tried to twist the question of suffering out of the hands of legalists and into the hands of poets. John Donne saw beyond justice, expressing in Sonnet XIV:

Batter my heart, three-person'd God. . . .
. . . for I,
Except you enthrall me, never shall be free,
Nor ever chaste, except you ravish me.

Like enthusiasts fresh from a seminary, Job's friends brought him a retributive theology they'd learned *about* God, but Job was mourning a relationship *with* God, which goes well beyond ideas, laws, concepts, traditions, and theological dissection. Within their rationalist restraints they could appeal only to the two lowest possible moral motivations: fear of greater punishment and hope of reward for capitulating. They simply could not comprehend a soul who has gone *beyond* conventional moral relationship; they couldn't fathom love.

When God arrives on the scene (quite late and quite unfairly in a whirlwind), he wrenches the situation completely out of the realms of justice and logic. "Where were you when I laid the foundations of the earth?" (Jb 38:4). Equivalently: Just who do you think you are? And who do you think I am? Should I screen my plans with you?"

What his words and the windstorm connote is the humbling Truth of Who God IS: overwhelmingly dynamic, too untamable to be captured in words or well-researched formulas or dogmas— the *mysterium tremendum* before whom we tremble, not in horror but in humbled fascination at a Presence so vibrant yet controlled, so intimidating yet welcoming. This is "the Lord of terrible aspect" who dwells in inaccessible light, the God the Epistle to the Hebrews describes when it says, "It is a dreadful thing to fall into the hands of the living God" (10:31).

God gives Job no rational answer. God gives *himself* as the answer. Once we have met the One who justifies all theologies, they are no longer necessary. At the end, God makes Job's friends offer sacrifice in Job's presence while Job prays for them, proving Job was right and they were wrong. Job has been innocent from the start, which never was the point of it all.

And Job doesn't say, "Ah, at last! You've proved your case!" Instead, he says, "In the past, I knew only what others told me, but now I have seen you with my own eyes" (Jb 42:5, *GNB*).

Forget Sherlock Holmes. We need the feisty, incandescent soul of Teresa of Avila, who reputedly handled God like a nun with her favorite pupil: "If you treat all your friends as badly as you treat me, I'm not surprised you have so few!" Especially in a culture that can't tolerate even inconvenience, it's nearly impossible to explain a love that endures no matter what. Meeting the true God is as incommunicable as falling in love. It's like drowning in light.

THE GOD OF JESUS CHRIST

The unequivocal symbol of the message of Christ is a crucifix—the corpse of a felon condemned for blasphemy and insurrection, drained of everything, for people who couldn't understand him. His nearly final words were, "Father, forgive them. They don't know what they're doing" (Lk 23:34). A convinced Christian looks at that figure and says, sincerely: "That is the greatest human being who ever lived, caught at the moment of his greatest triumph. He embodies everything almighty God intended human suffering to mean. I want to be like him."

It's important to deal first with a question that might seem peripheral to the problem of pain but is nonetheless intrusive. How could the eternal Son of God, by nature perfect and incapable of any state other than perfection, actually feel pain, abandonment, the razor edge of despair? How could he panic to the point of sweating blood in Gethsemane if he was in full possession of divine certitude (which has bedeviled these pages from the outset)? Was he merely quoting Psalm 22 when he cried out toward the end, "My God! My God, why have you abandoned me?" (Mt 27:46)? How could Someone enjoying the uncontaminated clarity of divine knowledge suffer doubt? And yet, ever since the very first ecumenical council at Nicea (325 C.E.), nearly all Christian churches up to today agree that Jesus Christ was both fully divine and fully human. But a (painful) constituent element of authentic humanity is *doubt*, living *without* precisely what distinguishes human from divine understanding.

In Philippians, Saint Paul offers at least a clue to how that could come about. At the incarnation, he says, the Son,

> who, although He existed in the form of God, did not regard equality with God a thing to be grasped, but emptied Himself, taking the form of a bond-servant, and being made in the likeness of men. (Phil 2:6–7, *NASB*)

In order to experience humanity fully, the Son freely surrendered any divine perquisites that would have made that impossible. To make an inadequate analogy, he became "amnesiac" about any understanding or clarity no human can enjoy. He learned who he truly was just as we must, step by step, and he bore the same uncertainty and calculated risks known by no other species but humans. On the cross, like Job, he felt genuine torment more profound than physical pain: the fear that, all along, he might have been wrong. Rather than rendering Jesus less trustworthy, such a surrender makes him even more reliable as a mentor. This is not some aloof deist god who set the world spinning and went away in a cloud of cosmic indifference. Nor some subjective god in our heads personifying goodness. Nor some energizing Life Force. This is a God who willingly stripped himself of all defenses to show us how humanity is "done."

Do many people who claim to be Christian think of that second self-emptying on the cross in moments when they claim to be Christian? In all those years of indoctrination, did anyone ever put the point that boldly? And if so, is the reality of that belief evident in our attitude to suffering? A crucifix is an obvious attempt to answer the problem of pain, yet it is just as bewildering to the strictly rational mind as God's answer to Job.

The prevailing justification for the cruelty of Calvary has been that Adam and Eve's flaunting of God's will was infinitely flagrant and thus could be assuaged only by the equally infinite slaughter of the divine Son. Concomitant with the too facile answer to original sin as the sole cause of suffering, the doctrine of atonement seems (to me) an overly simple explanation of the suffering of Calvary, which allegedly reverses the inevitability of original sin's effects.

The doctrine of atonement I accepted unquestioningly half my life now seems simply irreconcilable with the understanding of God that Jesus embodied in his preaching and in his dealing with sinners. He clearly taught that we, who are so prone to grudges, must forgive not seven times but seventy *times* seven times (Mt 18:2). That's 490 times, for *each* offender! "If you do not forgive others, then your Father will not forgive your transgressions" (Mt 6:15). "Whenever you stand praying, forgive, if you have anything against anyone, so that your Father who is in heaven will also forgive you your transgressions" (Mk 11:25). The God of my young years was (contradictorily) like the Pharisees Jesus excoriated, who burdens us with a demand for ready forgiveness he will not impose on himself (Lk 11:46).

Moreover, Jesus himself *never* made a repentant sinner crawl or demanded an exhaustive list of misdeeds or gave a penance (see Lk 7:36–50; 15:11–32; Jn 4:4–40; 8:1–11). The *only* people he didn't forgive were those who refused to accept their need for it (the Temple officials) or their worthiness of it (Judas). If we accept that Jesus is the definitive expression of the nature and will of God, how is it possible that the God Jesus revealed could hold a grudge longer than he will allow us to? How could he withhold forgiveness until a cruel blood ransom was offered in retribution? That might fit the bloodthirsty chthonic gods of primitive societies but not the father of the prodigal son. If we grant that God allowed humans to evolve incomplete, so that they could continually grow, how could he "infect" innocent infants with actual sinfulness as a punishment for a single human misdeed?

I don't deny the doctrine of atonement. I simply must honestly confess my ignorance of any argument that can justify it.

Why, then, did Jesus undergo such agony and indignity when God could have wiped out human imperfection and all past misdeeds with a simple snap of his will? The only-too-simple-sounding answer I find is: To show us how it's done. With dignity. And faith. And love.

If, indeed, there is merit in understanding the emergence of incomplete human intelligence and freedom as God's hope that creation will work its own way toward fulfillment—what Teilhard called the Omega Point—then Jesus was our model of dignity, faith, and love. He made his way to his destiny step by *uncertain* step. He bore desertion by his friends (Mt 26:56; Mk 14:50); and degradation and reviling from the crowds (Mt 27:20–25; 39–40; Mk 15:29), soldiers (Mk 15:16–20; Mt 27:27–31; Lk 22:63–64; 23:36; Jn 19:1–3), respected priests (Mk 14:65; 15:31–33; Mt 26:67–68), the Jewish puppet king (Lk 23:6–12), and even one of the outlaws crucified with him (Lk 23:39). And through it all, he stood silent (Mk 14:61; Mt 26:63; Lk 23:9; Jn 19:9).

But despite scriptural references to Jesus submitting "like a sheep, dumb before the shearers" (Is 53:7), this was not stoic, nerveless compliance. It was a willed acceptance of the Father's will—which was assuredly *unclear* to Jesus in Gethsemane: "'*Abba*, Father,' he said, 'everything is possible for you. Take this cup from me. Yet not what I will, but what you will'" (Mt 26:39). He said he was willing to take whatever his Father would choose to send. And he *meant* it. When he taught us to pray "thy will be done," he asked us to really mean it. Even when we don't understand. At the end, Jesus cried out close to despair. But at the last he freely surrendered his spirit. To his Father. And to us.

In the depths of his agonies Job could have legitimately cried out to God, "You, in your inaccessible heights! Do you have any more than an *idea* of how I feel? Can you even conceive how it *feels*?" And in Jesus, God can answer: "Yes. I can."

Do we often realize that the One utterly degraded on the cross is that same whirlwind God of Job? This blood-caked wretch is at the root of all "Is"!

> Where were you when I laid the earth's
>   foundation?
> Tell me, if you understand.
>
> Who marked off its dimensions? Surely you
>   know!
> Who stretched a measuring line across it?

> On what were its footings set,
>   or who laid its cornerstone—
>
> while the morning stars sang together
>   and all the angels shouted for joy?
>
> (Jb 38:4–7)

Can we move beyond the (again) easy-to-hand economic metaphor of debt and remission and see this (again) as not a matter of justice but a matter of love? Is that too bewildering to minds more exquisitely tuned to fairness than kindness? Jesus' passion—the crucifix—cries out: Is this *enough*? Does this finally show you how important you are to me? This is the same Yahweh who spread the wonders of the night sky to seduce us to wonderment, who steered us toward intelligence and forgiveness, who again and again stood patiently outside Israel's bordello.

This is the unspeakable greatness utterly degraded as the Suffering Servant Isaiah foresaw:

> He had no beauty or majesty to attract us to
>   him,
>   nothing in his appearance that we should
>   desire him.
> He was despised and rejected by men,
>   a man of sorrows, and familiar with
>   suffering.
> Like one from whom men hide their faces
>   he was despised, and we esteemed him not.
>
> (Is 53:2–4)

Even brute beasts can be brought to understand the basest motivations: fear and hope of reward, or even acquiescent group loyalty. But as far as we know, no other animals can respect and value law and order. And only those who allow themselves to weigh values *beyond* cold logic can transcend fixed rules to values like altruism and empathy, and even to the extreme that says,

"I will do the right thing, even if you kill me for it." But they are rare—those who actually embody our belief that humans are intended to be in the image of God.

Perhaps the profoundest message of the crucifix is not justice. Perhaps it's not even forgiveness. Perhaps its most overwhelming essence is generosity.

NOTES

Introduction

1. Mother Teresa of Calcutta, quoted in David Van Biema, "Mother Teresa's Crisis of Faith," *Time*, August 23, 2007, 39–40.

1. The Need for Certainty

1. Richard Dawkins, "Is Science a Religion?" *The Humanist* 57 (1997): 26–29.
2. René Descartes, *Discourse on the Method*, rule 1, trans. Donald A. Cress (Indianapolis: Hackett Publishing, 1999), 16.
3. Charles Dickens, *Hard Times* (New York: Signet, 1961), 1.
4. William J. O'Malley, *Meeting the Living God*, 3rd ed. (Mahwah, NJ: Paulist Press, 1998). Originally published in 1973.
5. Vatican I, *Dogmatic Constitution Dei Filius on the Catholic Faith*, chap. 4, "On Faith and Reason," in Denzinger-Schonmetzer, 3026.
6. Blaise Pascal, *Pensées*, trans. A. J. Krailsheimer (Harmondsworth: Penguin, 1995; originally published in 1967), 1670.
7. Martin Heidegger, *An Introduction to Metaphysics* (New Haven, CT: Yale University Press, 1959), 7.
8. Francisco Ayala, *Darwin and Intelligent Design* (Minneapolis: Fortress Press, 2006), 76.
9. G. K. Chesterton, *Orthodoxy* (New York: Image Books, 1959), 17.

2. Fugitives from Ourselves

1. Robert Johnson, *We* (San Francisco: Harper and Row, 1983), 3.
2. Abraham Maslow, *The Farther Reaches of Human Nature* (Harmondsworth: Penguin, 1976), 175.
3. W. H. Auden, "The Unknown Citizen," in *From Another Time* (New York: Random House, 1940).

4. Johann Neuhausler, *What Was It Like in Concentration Camp Dachau?* (Manz A. G., undated), 63. RM=Reichsmarks.

5. Henry David Thoreau, *Walden* (New York: Everyman's Library, 2006), chap. 1–A, no. 9.

6. Bruno Bettelheim, "Freud and the Soul," *New Yorker,* March 1, 1982, 52ff.

7. Ibid.

8. Abraham Heschel, *Who Is Man?* (Stanford, CA: Stanford University Press, 1965), 13.

9. Leo Rock, *Making Friends with Yourself* (Mahwah, NJ: Paulist Press, 1990), 103.

10. William James, *Varieties of Religious Experience: A Study in Human Nature* (New York: Longmans, Green, and Co., 1902), Lecture 1, "Religion and Neurology."

11. Viktor Frankl, *Man's Search for Meaning* (New York: Washington Square Press, 1963), 194.

12. Friedrich Nietzsche, *Twilight of the Idols,* trans. Thomas Common (New York: Dover, 2004), chap. 1, "Maxims and Arrows," no. 12.

13. Fyodor Dostoevsky, *The Brothers Karamazov* (Harmondsworth: Penguin, 1958), bk. 1, 298.

14. Frankl, *Man's Search for Meaning,* xiii.

15. James, *The Varieties of Religious Experience,* Lecture 3, "The Reality of the Unseen."

16. James Russell Lowell, quoted in ibid.

3. Feeling "At Home"

1. Dag Hammarskjöld, *Markings* (New York: Ballantine, 1987), 74. Originally published in Swedish in 1963.

2. Joseph Campbell, with Bill Moyers, *The Power of Myth* (New York: Doubleday, 1988), 112.

3. Sam Keen, *Hymns to an Unknown God* (New York: Bantam Books, 1994), 112.

4. Scripture and Myth

1. *The Jerome Biblical Commentary*, ed. Raymond Brown et al. (Englewood Cliffs, NJ: Prentice-Hall, 1968), 607.

2. See Burton H. Throckmorton, Jr., ed., *Gospel Parallels* (Camden, NJ: Nelson, 1992; originally published in 1957); William J. O'Malley, *Matthew, Mark, Luke, and You* (Notre Dame, IN: Ave Maria Press, 2004). Originally published Allen, TX: Thomas More, 1996.

3. William J. O'Malley, *The Voice of Blood* (Maryknoll, NY: Orbis Books, 1980).

5. The Christian Myth

1. See the excellent and quite readable summary in C. S. Lewis, *The Abolition of Man* (New York: Macmillan, 1947), 95–121.

2. For a treatment of Jesus' consciousness of his divinity, William J. O'Malley, *Meeting the Living God*, 3rd ed. (Mahwah, NJ: Paulist Press, 1998), 237–39. Originally published in 1973.

6. The Imperfect Church

1. Flannery O'Connor, *The Habit of Being* (New York: Farrar, Straus, Giroux, 1979), 124–25.

2. John Paul II, "Letter to the Reverend George V. Coyne, S.J., Director of the Vatican Observatory," in *Origins* 18, no. 23 (November 17, 1988): 377.

3. Cardinal Poupard, "Galileo: Report on Papal Commission Findings," *Origins* 22, no. 22 (November 12, 1992): 375.

4. Patty Crowley, "Confessions of a Birth Control Commission Catholic-Lay Member," *National Catholic Reporter* (December 17, 1993).

5. Gallup Poll, *Origins* 10, no. 17 (1981): 264.

6. This incident is recounted in Philip S. Kaufman, O.S.B., *Why You Can Disagree—and Remain a Faithful Catholic* (Bloomington, IN: Meyer-Stone, 1989), 70.

7. Peter Steinfels, *A People Adrift: The Crisis of the Roman Catholic Church in America* (New York: Simon and Schuster, 2003), 258.

8. USCCB, "The Nature and Scope of the Problem of Sexual Abuse of Minors by Catholic Priests and Deacons in the United States," a research study conducted by the John Jay College of Criminal Justice (Washington, DC: USCCB, 2004).

9. U.S. Department of Education, June 2004.

10. Pope Benedict XVI, "Responses to Some Questions Regarding Certain Aspects of the Doctrine on the Church" (ratified June 29, 2007).

7. But Science Says . . .

1. Richard Dawkins, "Is Science a Religion," *The Humanist* 57 (1997).

2. Archibald MacLeish, *J.B.*, acting edition (New York: Samuel French, 1958), 22.

3. William J. O'Malley, *Meeting the Living God,* 3rd ed. (Mahwah, NJ: Paulist Press, 1998). Originally published in 1973.

4. Dan-Erik Nilsson and Susanne Pelger, "A Pessimistic Estimate of the Time Required for an Eye to Evolve," *Proceedings of the Royal Society of London*, series B, vol. 256 (1994), 53–58.

5. Annie Dillard, *Teaching a Stone to Talk* (New York: Harper and Row, 1982), 89.

6. Carl Sagan, *The Dragons of Eden* (New York: Ballantine Books, 1978), 14–16.

7. Richard Dawkins, *River out of Eden* (New York: Harper Collins, 1995), 96.

8. Kenneth R. Miller, *Finding Darwin's God: A Scientist's Search for Common Ground between God and Evolution* (New York: Harper Perennial, 2002), 238–39. Originally published in 1999.

9. Stephen Hawking, *A Brief History of Time* (New York: Bantam Books, 1998), 121. Originally published in 1988.

10. Miller, *Finding Darwin's God*, 252.

11. Richard Dawkins, *The Blind Watchmaker: Why the Evidence of Evolution Reveals a Universe without Design* (New York: W. W. Norton, 1986), 141.

12. Dawkins, *River out of Eden*, 96.

8. Suffering

1. Erik Erikson, *Identity* (New York: W. W. Norton, 1968).

2. Viktor Frankl, *Man's Search for Meaning* (New York: Washington Square Press, 1963), 106–7.

3. Cf. C. S. Lewis, *Perelandra* (New York: Macmillan, 1994; originally published in 1943), which reimages the Fall on the planet Venus; instead of fruit the Enemy offers the first female a mirror.

4. Simone Weil, *Waiting for God* (New York: Harper and Row, 1952), 120–21.

SELECT BIBLIOGRAPHY

Unless otherwise noted, all scripture quotations are from the New International Version.

Auden, W. H. "The Unknown Citizen." In *From Another Time*. New York: Random House, 1940.

Ayala, Francisco. *Darwin and Intelligent Design*. Minneapolis: Fortress Press, 2006.

Bettelheim, Bruno. "Freud and the Soul." *New Yorker,* March 1, 1982.

Brown, Raymond, et al. *The Jerome Biblical Commentary*. Englewood Cliffs, NJ: Prentice-Hall, 1968.

Campbell, Joseph, with Bill Moyers. *The Power of Myth*. New York: Doubleday, 1988.

Chesterton, G. K. *Orthodoxy*. New York: Image Books, 1959.

Dawkins, Richard. "Is Science a Religion?" *The Humanist* 57 (1997).

———. *The Blind Watchmaker: Why the Evidence of Evolution Reveals a Universe without Design*. New York: W. W. Norton, 1986.

———. *River out of Eden*. New York: HarperCollins, 1995.

Descartes, René. *Discourse on the Method*. Translated by Donald A. Cress. Indianapolis: Hackett Publishing, 1999.

Crowley, Patty. "Confessions of a Birth Control Commission Catholic-Lay Member." *National Catholic Reporter* (December 17, 1993).

Dickens, Charles, *Hard Times*. New York: Signet, 1961.

Dillard, Annie. *Teaching a Stone to Talk*. New York: Harper and Row, 1982.

Dostoevsky, Fyodor. *The Brothers Karamazov*. Harmondsworth: Penguin, 1958.

Eliade, Mircea, *The Sacred and the Profane*. New York: Harcourt Brace, 1959.

Erikson, Erik. *Identity*. New York: W. W. Norton, 1968.

Frankl, Viktor. *Man's Search for Meaning*. New York: Washington Square Press, 1963.

Hammarskjöld, Dag. *Markings*. New York: Ballantine, 1987. Originally published in Swedish in 1963.

Hawking, Stephen, *A Brief History of Time*. New York: Bantam Books, 1998. Originally published in 1988.

Heidegger, Martin, *An Introduction to Metaphysics*. New Haven, CT: Yale University Press, 1959.

Heschel, Abraham. *Who Is Man?* Stanford, CA: Stanford University Press, 1965.

James, William. *The Varieties of Religious Experience: A Study in Human Nature*. New York: Longmans, Green, and Co., 1902.

John Paul II. "Letter to the Reverend George V. Coyne, S.J., Director of the Vatican Observatory." *Origins* 18, no. 23 (November 17, 1988).

Johnson, Robert. *We*. San Francisco: Harper and Row, 1983.

Kaufman, Philip S., O.S.B. *Why You Can Disagree—and Remain a Faithful Catholic*. Bloomington, IN: Meyer-Stone, 1989.

Keen, Sam. *Hymns to an Unknown God*. New York: Bantam Books, 1994.

Lewis, C. S. *The Abolition of Man*. New York: Macmillan, 1947.

———. *Perelandra*. New York: Macmillan, 1994. Originally published in 1943)

MacLeish, Archibald. *J.B.* Acting edition. New York: Samuel French, 1958.

Maslow, Abraham. *The Farther Reaches of Human Nature*. Harmondsworth: Penguin, 1976.

Miller, Kenneth R. *Finding Darwin's God: A Scientist's Search for Common Ground between God and Evolution*. New York: Harper Perennial, 2002. Originally published in 1999.

Neuhausler, Johann. *What Was It Like in Concentration Camp Dachau?* Manz A. G., undated.

Nietzsche, Friedrich, *Twilight of the Idols*. Translated by Thomas Common. New York: Dover, 2004.

O'Connor, Flannery. *The Habit of Being*. New York: Farrar, Straus, Giroux, 1979.

O'Malley, William J. *Matthew, Mark, Luke, and You*. Notre Dame, IN: Ave Maria Press, 2004. Originally published Allen, TX: Thomas More, 1996.

———. *Meeting the Living God*. 3rd edition. Mahwah, NJ: Paulist Press, 1998. Originally published in 1973.

———. *The Voice of Blood*. Maryknoll, NY: Orbis Books, 1980.

Pascal, Blaise, *Pensées*. Translated by A. J. Krailsheimer. Harmondsworth: Penguin, 1995. Originally published in 1967.

Rock, Leo. *Making Friends with Yourself*. Mahwah, NJ: Paulist Press, 1990.

Sagan, Carl. *The Dragons of Eden*. New York: Ballantine Books, 1978.

Steinfels, Peter. *A People Adrift: The Crisis of the Roman Catholic Church in America.* New York: Simon and Schuster, 2003.

Thoreau, Henry David. *Walden.* New York: Everyman's Library, 2006.

Throckmorton, Burton H., Jr., ed. *Gospel Parallels.* Camden, NJ: Nelson, 1992. Originally published in 1957.

Weil, Simone. *Waiting for God.* New York: Harper and Row, 1952.